Vegan Cookbook for Beginners

The Essential Vegan Cookbook – Easy, Healthy and Delicious Vegan Recipes That You'll Love

Table of Contents

Introduction

We love food and we love cooking! This cookbook is designed for people like us, who love food and cooking who also want to expand their menu by venturing out on a new path to test the waters. You might be curious to know more about Vegan cooking. You might be thinking about becoming a Vegan. You might be thinking about adapting a Vegan diet to suit your already established needs. Some people want to learn more about Vegan cooking for health reasons. Others, for ethical or financial. However you shake it, we will tell you how to make it. There are no rules that come with this book.

This introduction cookbook to Vegan cooking is packed with recipes that will astonish and surprise you. While eating Vegan is a new idea developed over the past century, the truth is that many foods our parents and grandparents have eaten over the years have had Vegan overtones. Despite this not being the purpose of the dishes, this cookbook is composed with new and traditional recipes in mind. So for example, a Vegan main dish you have never tried before can be complemented by grandpa's roasted potatoes. The combination is a way of bringing Vegan food into the comfort food zone (where is often is even though we are not aware of it).

The blending of both the traditional and the new does not detract from Vegan dishes. It adds to them! It demonstrates to one's mind (and mouth) that Veganism is a natural extension of the human diet. But that does not mean it is not new. On the contrary, Vegan cooking requires using kitchen ingredients often overlooked. Some are overshadowed by other more popular ingredients. Others are newly made to assist Vegan cooking. The goal at hand is to expand the reach of Vegan foods until cooking anything is possible, which is a lot of fun to think about for anyone who loves cooking.

You can eat Vegan once a week or make one Vegan dish a night to add variety to your family dinners. You may be looking for a go-to Vegan cookbook easy to turn to when you have Vegan friends over for dinner. It is not a secret that veganism is becoming altogether more common. A large swath of the younger generations are turning to it and in turn, some of the older ones are, too.

We can see all kinds of signs, from the rise in vegan cafes to menus in traditional restaurants that now offer a limited selection of Vegan options. The same is true of grocery stores. Many of them now have tailored Vegan sections. But eating Vegan food is one thing and cooking it is another.

Cooking Vegan dishes is a bit of a wild ride because it requires unlearning a lot of what you have learned goes on in a kitchen. For those of you who are just getting your feet wet, this book is filled with Vegan recipes that are among the most simple to make. That does not mean we have not compiled adventurous recipe ideas that will inspire news ways to explore and enjoy your favorite foods -- we have! You will find how to make a number of familiar dishes -- like pizza -- only you will make them like you have never made them before.

In addition, we have included information for you to read and learn what Veganism is and the various ways it is used. We discuss the benefits of eating a Vegan based diet, all of which would not make a lot of sense without including suggestions for integrating a Vegan diet into your life. So, we have included information on that as well. To entirely dive in does take a measure of effort. Nearly all Vegan dishes -- outside the scope of those old standard dishes that are Vegan but never intended to be -- require a few items one will is not likely to have on hand. Butter, meat, oil, milk and cheese   substitutes along with certain grains, such as quinoa, will need to be purchased. It is going to run smoothly if one refers to the list we provide in a later chapter.

We have tips on how to smoothly navigate the transition to a vegan diet as well as tips on sustaining the diet, including information that addresses unavoidable issues such as dining out. It is better to have a rough idea what you are up against before you find yourself in the middle of a crowded restaurant with a group of friends. Lastly, the core of the book is made from a tapestry of recipes that are not only easy to make but are all too familiar. We are not kidding! Included is everything from pizza to hamburger recipes not to mention some to die for desserts! First, let's go to the next chapter and examine what exactly is meant when we say: *Vegan.*

Chapter 1: What is Vegan?

A Vegan diet does not include any animal or animal products, including meat, milk, and eggs. The reasons behind the diet can be expressed both through the diet and as a philosophy. This means some folks simply eat Vegan diet because it is what is best for them. Others eat a Vegan diet because it aligns with a philosophy that does not support the commodification of animals. Their argument is that raising animals for slaughter is cruel.

Beyond this, the Vegan world breaks into several more subcategories. We will not cover them all. We will instead outline the history of the Vegan movement and some of the different ideologies that go along with it as to give you a basic understanding of how and why the movement came to r fruition. Along with this, we will point out some of the health benefits of a Vegan diet, including the ways a Vegan diet contributes to the health of the plant.

To understand the reasons behind its sudden appearance on the horizon we only have to step back in time a short distance. One day no one was eating Vegan food and the next, there were Vegan cafes popping up along the streets. As with most any diet one crosses paths with, each toutes a different outstanding feature that is inextricably linked to a specific promised outcome. The most popular of these promises is of course weight loss.

The vegan diet is unique in that it is not comprised with a singular goal in mind. Eating a vegan diet addresses a vast range of potential outcomes. Health is one. The diet reduces the risk of certain diseases. Weight loss is one. No surprise there. Improved health is another. No surprise there, either. But the vegan diet goes further than this... and there is your *surprise!*

There is a positive and direct and measurable environmental impact that a Vegan diet contributes toward making. This not only sets the Vegan diet apart from other diets, it demonstrates the Vegan diet marks the beginning of a new chapter for mankind. What one eats and what time one eats is largely the result of geographic location. In sun soaked regions, such as Italy and Spain families often do not have dinner until 9 or 10 at night. In wind swept canals tracing the Netherlands, by the time 9 or 10pm has rolled around, folks are finishing their meals.

In the same way geography plays a role on what time we eat, for years location has impacted what foods we have access to. Again, if we look at Europe, the colder, northern regions spanning from Ireland to France and Germany where it is common to consume a greater amount of bread and potatoes. Main dishes are often smothered in glorious butter based sauces. In contrast, pasta and olive oil based dishes define the warm southern lands. This has shaped food traditions and within that scope, it has shaped what roles we give each ingredient.

No matter one's motive, Vegan cooking takes on traditional menus and rethinks them. The outcome is one of the reasons why cooking a Vegan meal demands that we readdress the roles given to the foods humans have been consuming over the last centuries.

Type Casting Food Roles

Over the past century, fruits and vegetables have been assigned specific roles to play. Carrots accompany lunches. They are given supporting roles as side dishes next to dinner entrees. Carrots are typecast in this way as are most of the foods we eat. While cooking Vegan playfully requires we eliminate many staple ingredients we have grown accustomed to cooking with, at the same time it instructs us to use vegetables, like carrots, in ways we had never considered.

This change of the rules demands a change of the roles we have (often without even knowing it) given to the everyday foods we keep in our kitchens. For example, carrots can be used to make smoothies, burgers, soups, salads and desserts. Yet they are most often not used as a side dish. Vegan cooking inspires we open the floodgates to potential uses of plant based foods.

Political versus Lifestyle

Now, there is a lot that can be said about Veganism. For many, it is seen as an extreme diet. But that is only true if one looks at it through a narrow scope. Veganism is somewhat complex because there are a number of reasons why it is practiced, just as there are a number of different ways it can be practiced.

Just like Buddhism can either be a philosophy or religion, Veganism can either be political or a preferred (healthy) lifestyle choice. The reasons Veganism falls into the political sphere is because the animal food industry is mired with problems. Not eating meat devoids the industry from making money. Hormone additives, over breeding and overuse of antibiotics, are some of the problems associated with cruelty to livestock.

Environmental issues surface as part of the web of problems, too. Animals produce methane which is linked to the rise in CO2 in the atmosphere and it is hypothesized is the major cause of global warming. If we curbed the amount of meat we consume then a domino effect would happen. Fewer cattle would be raised and therefore less methane would be released. A person who refrains from consuming any form of meat for with this as their purpose is practicing what is often called Ethical Veganism.

Ethical reasons for eating a vegan diet risen with alongside the realities faced by global warming. But global warming is not the single driving force behind this movement. Some ethical Vegans reach further than a plant based diet by refusing to buy anything made from animal, including clothing. In this way, ethical Veganism can be too demanding for a majority of individuals to follow. On the other hand eating Vegan has proved to be popular to the extent it has become something of a trend.

Vegan cafes boomed in 2010. This was the same year Veganism was recognized by the mainstream by governments, where in some countries Vegan food labels were affixed to food items in major markets and food stores. There is no doubt this falls into lockstep with the millennial generation. They more than anyone have come of age faced with more than the hypothesis of environmental concerns. For them, the icebergs are not maybe going to melt -- they are melting. A Vegan lifestyle allows them to participate against the wave of complacency by generations that preceded them. At the same time, it acknowledges that times are a changin'.

The advent of the computer marks the beginning of a new age. The Big Data era and technologies that come with it are altering traditions. As I write this, advances in science have inspired scientists and entrepreneurs to take steps toward growing meat that is entirely grown within a controlled lab environment. Products such as mayonnaise are already on the shelves. It is becoming more and more difficult to identify the difference between what is "real" and what is "lab grown" This is exciting for those getting into Vegan cooking. Now is the time there are (as you will learn in a later chapter) a large variety of viable products that are excellent substitutes to use in Vegan cooking.

These inventions have enabled the millennial generation to play a vital role in maintaining a Vegan lifestyle that acts against the accepted patterns of generations past. Their parent's generation, too are no strangers to the vegan movement which surfaced for the first time in the 1840's. In the United States, it was not until over 100 years later the 1960's counter culture movement winded the flames.

This was partly driven by Rachel Carson's hugely popular books, *Silent Spring*. First published in 1962, *Silent Spring* offered a convincing argument that pesticides used on foods were directly to blame for a number of detrimental health issues. The book's release angered the chemical industry who stood accused of not only creating the chemicals being used on food but manipulating facts as to mislead the public about the safety of their use.

Reaction to the book was widespread. As it grew, so too did the 60's counter movement's contempt for big industry. Many individuals looked for alternatives to eating industrial farmed foods. The animal farming industry was not free from the suspicion. Soon, a vegetarian movement began to blossom but that is not when the vegetarian movement started.

Veganism got its start before the height of the Industrial Revolution yet it was during that time when scientific research acknowledged there to be two different types of vegetarian. The turn of the century 1900's saw a massive rise in the industrialization of foods as well as man-made items. The question began to come to the minds of a few people about this practice. What kind of diet are we eating if we consume products from a species that has been treated as if it were anything but a living, breathing being.

Ethical Veganism entirely devotes itself to this idea. At the core of their argument is not concern for the consumer but the animals which are sentient beings. This means they are endowed with a similar array of emotions as humans and killing and eating them is simply, therefore, unconscionable.

Culinary Happiness

No matter your reasons for wanting to delve into the world of Vegan cooking we believe the more menu options you have, the richer your kitchen will become. We believe you do not have to buy exotic imported foods or additional new appliances in order to earn gold stars for your culinary efforts. We point this out to take some of the focus off the ethical reasons a Vegan diet is a good choice. Eating Vegan is a good choice regardless of this truth. It is excellent for the health of those with certain health conditions. We will cover this more in the following chapter. For now, we want to keep the spotlight on Vegan cooking as a way to explore new kitchen adventures.

Kitchen adventures give birth to a love of food, eating and imagination -- all of which are the key ingredients to making mouth watering dishes. That, mixed with a dash of understanding behind the tradition of eating together -- which calls on us to bring people together. Being together also nourishes the body and the spirit. Not that that long ago lived a generation of folks for whom meals were the result of what came from the garden.

Depending on the season, those foods would have consisted of anything from tomatoes, onions, cucumbers, zucchini, and so on. During that same era, most poultry and red meat came from a neighboring farm and the fish from a nearby stream, sea or lake. All of these foods have one thing in common. They are what we now label as Whole Food which are also connected with health. Vegan cooking has a number of health benefits of its own.

Chapter 2: Benefits of Being a Vegan

Health and Veganism

Eating a vegan diet reduces heart disease. The diet is high in fiber. It draws a number of vitamins and minerals from the variety of sources included in the diet -- and there are many. As you will see in the chapters to follow, the amount of substitute options are extensive. This was not always true. If you are just now coming to the Vegan diet, you are fortunate! Before the Vegan boom of 2010, cooking Vegan required looking far and wide for the tools needed. Even major cities only had a handful of healthfood stores on hand. This meant a person usually had to go out of their way to shop. Most of the stores at that time had a limited range of options available to sell and certainly lacked a mixture of brands.

As stores like Whole Foods started to spring up, their rise in popularity demonstrated an alternative health food source was of interest to the general public who were there spending not just money but paying more for their food to assure it comes from a viable source. The underlying health benefits from eating so-called "clean foods" rests on proven truths and theories. Regardless if the theories are right, eating food that emerges from an environmentally sustainable farm is arguably worth the few extra bucks. Assume that eating such foods impacts one's overall health certainly is worth paying a few more dollars for.

Nonetheless, the most healthy food is the food that comes straight from the garden. After the garden the should ideally be consumed in their natural state. These are fresh foods such as are fresh fruits, vegetables, legumes, grains. They are at the core of every healthy diet. It will not surprise you the so-called Golden Generation, those born during the early to mid 1900's, often lived long, healthy lives -- despite drinking and smoking cigarettes.

The Golden Generation diet consisted of locally grown produce. Often families did not use the grocery store. It was far more common to grow one's own vegetables and can extra tomatoes and corn and other foods to last through the winter. As we fast forward to today, packaged and processed foods are too often packed with fats, cheap oils, sodium, refined sugars and artificial sweeteners along with refined carbohydrates and grains. Reconnecting to foods that come from the Earth. Reconnecting to generations from the past. Reconnecting around the dinner table with your family. Reconnecting around the dinner table with your friends. The ritual of sitting around a dinner table and sharing stories and laughter is alone nourishing. When done together over a plate of steaming warm food, it's heaven.

Whole Foods are foods that are consumable in their natural state. This means they have not been processed or altered with anything artificial. No added color, sugar, or chemicals. When we talk about Whole Foods we are talking about a diet that is made from veggies, fruits, spices, oils, nuts, and seeds. Generally speaking, whole foods are not cereals or anything that comes in a box. No candy bars, no ice cream -- nothing with ingredients you cannot pronounce. If you cannot say it, you probably should think twice before eating it!

This is not to say there are no packaged and processed foods that can be included as part of a healthy diet. They are good to consider buying and keeping around the house and include a variety of items: Frozen Vegetables, Frozen Fruits, Quick Cooking Brown Rice, Canned Beans, Kitchen-Ready Tomatoes, Grains: oatmeal, buckwheat, barley, brown rice, cracked wheat, quinoa, and millet, Dried Fruit, Raw Nuts, Seeds & Nut-Seed Butter, Spices and Seasoning, Herbs -- because we all need a little zest in life!

Vegan cooking will, at the least, introduce one to alternative options. For example, ingredients like quinoa are often utilized in Vegan cooking. This is true about breakfast. Lunch, snacks and dinners. Quinoa is 100% protein grain has been growing in popularity and there is a good reason why. It is light, easy to cook, and mixes well with a variety of foods and flavors because it has not overarching taste of its own. It grows in the high mountain of Peru and in a similar climate in Colorado. Quinoa originates from the Andean region of South America, where people have been farming & eating it 3000 to 4000 years. The Incas saw the crop as sacred and referring to it as "mother of all grains".

Environmental Health and Your Health

Another benefit from eating a vegan diet is that you are directly impacting the environment in a positive way. Industrial farming takes a toll on the Earth in a number of ways. Overgrazing by animals causes soil erosion. This in turn causes the ruination of biodiversity and is linked as a cause of climate change. The same is true when water sources are overfished. The human desire to extending our reach by plucking out as many fish as we can rather than limiting ourselves to taking only as many fish as can be reproduced in a year's time, depletes fish stocks. This in turn causes the ecosystem of the ocean to become out of balance.

Eliminating animal and animal bi products from one's diet decreases the demand for these products that cover our grocery shelves. Many who subscribe to the Vegan lifestyle see this as a direct way to save the planet. The impact of such an effort cannot be overstated. Animal products are used in all kinds of ways that are hidden.

The average consumer does not know for instance that food additives can be derived from animal products. For example, E120, E322, E422, E 471, E542, E631, E901 and E904. Ground insects are used to make carmine, a natural dye used to give a red color to many food products. Gelatin is a thickening agent comes from the skin, bones and connective tissues of a wide range of animals. Isinglass is a gelatin-like substance is derived from fish bladders. Products that are enriched with omega-3s are not Vegan since most omega-3s come from fish. Omega-3s derived from algae are vegan alternatives and most vitamin D3 is derived from fish oil or the lanolin found in sheep's wool. These are just a few examples. We provide a detailed list in the next chapter for you.

Knowing all this, one should conclude that eating Vegan is something you can feel good about. It is a meaningful decision that takes dedication; as such it is beneficial to one's overall life-health. When we act in ways that make us feel better, we are better.

Chapter 3: Vegan OK Foods vs Vegan Not OK Foods

As mentioned in the earlier chapter, you will likely be surprised in what foods animal products are hidden. Most of us only think about animal products as the direct meat source itself and overlook the vast ways animal bi products make their way into our lives.

While this chapter begins by outlining the foods off limits for Vegan cooking, we do not want you to be discouraged. Keep reading! As you do, you will come to an even longer list outlining what foods are okay to consume. Along with them, you will find an extensive list of food substitutes. So, while you may be panicked -- don't! Cooking Vegan means not using milk (for instance) but instead, you are given a list of alternatives to try using. This is where the fun begins and new ideas begin to usher themselves forward.

Foods that are NOT OK:

1. Meat and all animal products: Meat: Beef, lamb, pork, veal, horse, organ meat, wild meats.
2. Poultry: Chicken, turkey, goose, duck.
3. Fish and seafood: All types of fish, anchovies, shrimp, squid, scallops, calamari, mussels, crab, fish sauce.
4. Dairy: Milk, yoghurt, cheese, butter, cream, ice cream.
5. Eggs: From chickens, quails, ostriches and fish.
6. Bee products: Honey, bee pollen, royal jelly.

Now, let's cover where animal products show up that you might not realize.

- Food additives can be derived from animal products. Examples include E120, E322, E422, E 471, E542, E631, E901 and E904.
- Carmine: You will be happy to know that ground insects are used to make carmine, a natural dye used to give a red color to many food products.
- Gelatin is a thickening agent comes from the skin, bones and connective tissues of a wide range of animals.
- Isinglass: This gelatin-like substance is derived from fish bladders. It's often used in the making of beer or wine.
- Natural flavorings.

- Omega-3 fatty acids: Many products that are enriched with omega-3s are not vegan, since most omega-3s come from fish. Omega-3s derived from algae are vegan alternatives.
- Shellac: Used most often as a dessert glaze, shellac's origins may surprise you -- it is a substance secreted by the female lac insect.
- Vitamin D3: Most vitamin D3 is derived from fish oil or the lanolin found in sheep's wool.

Foods that are OK:

1. Plant-based foods including fruits, vegetables, grains, beans, nuts, and seeds.
2. Vitamin D2 and D3 from lichen are vegan alternatives.

Commonly asked questions:

Can I eat bread?

No. However, there is a spectrum at play here. Some people choose to keep eggs in their diet. This practice is called *Lacto-vegetarians*. Others are fine with eating eggs but exclude milk and dairy products from their diet. This practice is called *ovo-vegetarianism*.

It is important to note that breads are not excluded from these diet regimens unless they contain animal ingredients. And, we have added a wealth of information that will guide you through egg and milk substitutes you can use to bake yourself bread to eat that keeps you well in line with the vegan code of conduct.

Is wheat Vegan? What about flour?

Generally speaking: Yes.

What is Tempeh?

Tempeh is made by deep-frying fermented soybeans.

Grocery Shopping

A basic Vegan shopping list will look made from a list of substitutes. Milk Substitutes: including any unsweetened organic, non-dairy milk like rice, almond, hemp, cashew, oat or soymilk. Butter Substitutes. Cheese Substitutes. Egg Substitutes. Meat Substitutes. Sweeteners. Condiments. Nuts, Seeds & Dried Fruits.

Milk Substitutes

Any unsweetened organic, non-dairy milk like rice, almond, hemp, cashew, oat or soymilk are excellent milk substitutes. Hemp milk is a complete protein. This means it contains all of the amino acids necessary for optimal health. A single serving of hemp milk provides an entire day's recommended intake of omega 3 fats. It is mild tasting and goes well with cereals.

Soymilk has a nutrition profile most like dairy milk. It is the highest in protein sporting 8 and 11 grams per cup. Soy milk is good in coffee and helps smoothies achieve their silky, smooth consistency.

Almond milk is low in calories and sugar than most non-dairy milks. It also contains monounsaturated fats, which are heart healthy. Almond milk separates when heated. It works best in cereals and smoothies.

Cashew milk is creamy and sweet but can be high in sugar. One might want to opt for buying the unsweetened brand. It works well with smoothies.

Rice milk is non-allergenic which sets it apart from a lot of these options. It is the low protein and is high in sugar and calories. Depending on what your goals are, this may or may not be the milk for you.

Oat milk offers fiber and protein, with 4 grams per serving. However, it is on the higher end in terms of sugar and calories.

Fast Facts:
1. Almond, hemp, soy, coconut and rice milk can easily be used in baked goods.
2. All non-dairy milk are vegan and lactose-free.
3. There are brands of non-dairy milk that incorporate added fats and sweeteners including cane juice and brown rice syrup.

Butter Substitutes

We recommend Coconut Oil (see Chapter 5) because many butter substitutes that are popular vegan butter options are made from processed foods, including fats extracted in the process of making a whole food and oil.

Cheese Substitutes

There are many vegan cheese substitutes on the market but always remember these are processed foods. Nutritional yeast (see Chapter 5) has a similar salty, nutty taste like parmesan. This makes it a great cheese replacement for everything from baked macaroni and cheese to cheesy popcorn. It is great on pasta and pizza, too.

Egg Substitutes

There are many commercial egg substitutes on the market:

Ground flax seed eggs
1. Whisk two tablespoons of ground flaxseed with six tablespoons of water until fluffy.
2. Place the mixture in the refrigerator for 10 minutes to thicken.

Chia Seed Eggs
1. Whisk one tablespoon chia seeds with 3 tablespoons of water.
2. Mix and let sit for fifteen minutes.

Cornstarch Eggs:
- Combine two tablespoons of cornstarch with three tablespoons of water.

Arrowroot Eggs:
- Combine two tablespoons of Arrowroot with three tablespoons of water

Chickpea Flour Eggs:
- Whisk three tablespoons of Chickpea flour with three tablespoons of water

Applesauce and Bananas:
- Smash up or blend about a half a banana or 1/4 cup applesauce to use as an egg replacer in baked goods such as muffins, pancakes or yeast-free quick breads.

Tofu: For two eggs:
- Blend 1/4 cup silken tofu until tofu is smooth and creamy.

Aquafaba (Aquafaba is the liquid from cooked chickpeas):
1. Three tablespoons equals 1 egg white.
2. Whip the liquid until foamy not over whipped with a hand mixer.

Meat Substitutes

- Vegan chicken, crumbles and veggie burgers you should look for in your local health food store.
- Gardein Fresh & Frozen options are sometimes a great option. You will find brands you like and dislike. Be playful!
- Field Roast Sausages – If you are craving a frankfurter or sausage, I think Field Roast tastes the best.
- Look for vegan bacon.

Sweeteners

- Stevia for coffee and tea
- Maple Syrup
- Blackstrap Molasses
- Zulka – 100% Vegan Sugar

Condiments

- Vegan Mayonnaise
- Ketchup
- Mustard

Nuts, Seeds & Dried Fruits

- Nuts are high in protein and can be added to almost any meal.
- Seeds and dried fruits make wonderful toppings for oatmeal and salads.
- Hemp seeds, ground flax seeds and chia seeds contain a great balance of omega-6 and omega-3s.
- Flaxseeds.

Vegetables

You know where they are and what they are. The only advice I can offer is to try and buy organic especially foods with thin outer skins.

Herbs

Parsley, cilantro, garlic, ginger and mint when possible for additional flavoring.

Proteins

Lentils, Tofu, Beans, Quinoa, Soy, Chickpeas, Green Peas, Artichokes, Hemp Seeds, Chia Seeds, Oatmeal, Pumpkin Seeds, Hemp Milk, Edamame, Spinach, Black Eyed Peas, Broccoli, Asparagus, Green Beans, Almonds, Spirulina, Tahini, Nutritional Yeast, Peanut Butter, and Amaranth.

Chickpeas

High in protein. Mash them up with a little vegan mayo and cucumber together with a slice of bread with avocado and sprouts. Add them to soups and salads.

Whole Grains

Grain consists of three parts: the bran, germ, and endosperm.

Rice

Look for rise that still has a side hull and bran. The side hulls and brans are rich in protein, thiamine, calcium, magnesium, selenium, fiber and potassium.

Farro

A healthy whole grain that is popular in Italy. Farro is an excellent source of protein, fiber and nutrients like magnesium and iron.

Additional Grains

Barley, Millet, Teff, Wild Rice, Wheat, Buckwheat, Amaranth, Buckwheat, Bulgur, Kamut, Oats, Freekeh, and Spelt are also considered whole grains.

Legumes

Lentils & Beans are a high source of protein and iron.

Cupboard & Refrigerator

Nutritional Yeast, Apple Cider Vinegar, Chickpeas, Cannellini Beans, Black Beans, Grains, Sun-dried Tomatoes, Olives, Organic ground tomatoes, Whole-wheat flour, Artichokes,

Chickpea Flour, Seasonings Red Pepper flakes, Sriracha (hot sauce), Rice Vinegar, Dried herbs, Chipotle, Chili Powder, Cumin, Onion Powder, Ground Ginger.

Yogurt

Any non-dairy yogurt including soy, almond or coconut.

Vegetable Broth

Useful for many of your soups and stews.

Pasta & Noodles

Whole grain!

Chapter 4: Transitions -- Tips for Eating Out

The Rise of the Vegan cafe makes eating Vegan outside the home possible – very possible -- and fun to sustain. Of course, this is true with a few exceptions depending on where one lives. Rural areas that already have too few cafes to choose from might cause a person to have a hard time adapting their Vegan eating habits – but that does not means it is impossible. Almost everywhere serves plant based options. Stick with salads when you are not certain.

When we get down to the nitty gritty, those in rural communities where options are limited do miss out. The truth is that most all Vegan cafes will offer you a variety of interesting options. A run of the mill cafe will give you what you are used to. At the end of the day it is not as much fun but going out is better than staying in! So, go out with your friends and family! And don't lose sight of the bigger picture. If you are reading this book, it's because you are on the brink of creating your own Vegan masterpieces – not eat out.

If in a number of cities, you will find Vegan cafes and a large amount of restaurants offer at the very least a few Vegan items on their menu. This is purely in response to the popularity in eating Vegan. At the end of 2010, eating Vegan blossomed in a big way. Cafes sprouted like weeds throughout the most populated cities and university towns. Then, Vegan eating trickled into the consciousness of the general public, many of whom had no idea what it was all about soon did.

Now, a lot of folks who are not Vegan still participate through buying Vegan foods to take home and try because about the same time the boom in eating Vegan happened, grocery stores were getting asked about carrying Vegan foods. The shelves have slowly become stocked with a spattering of items. And, then more items. And, then more still! Some of them were high quality. Some not. It has taken time for brands that people most like to make it to the front of the shelves, but it is nonetheless happening.

Today, someone wanting a Vegan meal for dinner does not have to look far. Another reason Vegan food spread quickly is because much of it did not need to. The idea only had to spread. Once folks knew what Vegan meant, they could easily label what they had in stock as either Vegan or non-Vegan. Salads and vegetarian meals may have already qualified as Vegan despite a cafe realizing they offer any such diet on site.

This again is why eating out should not be much of a problem. Even if a person enters a steakhouse there is a high probability they can order something entirely Vegan for their meal.

Chapter 5: Cooking Vegan: Tips and Tricks

One of the dynamic aspects about eating Vegan is the diet's zest for imitation. You never have to entirely go without what you most love in terms of foods and food flavors. Vegan chefs are all the time exploring alternative ways to mask this exchange so the person eating cannot tell the Vegan content from the "real thing".

Science is on the bandwagon, too. As mentioned in an earlier chapter, labs all over the world are competing to grow meat and other imitation products that taste, feel, smell and look like the original. As they succeed, incredible tasting milk, egg and meat substitutes are being offered to those who want to cook Vegan based meals.

As a person interested in making Vegan dishes, you will be far ahead of the game knowing some of the items often used in Vegan cooking that aid in replicating original dishes. In this next section, we do our best to explain how some of the substitutes are used and when it is better to use one rather than the other. We also added a list of Fast Facts that highlight information you will find useful in deciding whether or not the product is right for you.

Phyllo Dough or Puff Pastry

We think of puffy pastries and let's face it, we are too busy devouring to think about them beyond their intoxicating taste. More than one Vegan chef has made the mistake of using the terms *puff pastry* and *phyllo dough* interchangeably, as if they are the same thing.

They're not at all the same thing. It is helpful to know the difference particularly for those who have a propensity for baking!

Fast Facts:
1. Phyllo dough is lower in fat than puff pastry.
2. Puff pastry dough is made by placing cold slices of butter between layers of pastry dough, at which point it is rolled out and folded, over and over until there many layers of dough infused with rich, fatty butter. Croissants, for example, are one of the deliciously well-known baked goods whose genesis is puff pastry.
3. One can make phyllo dough as calorie intense as puff pastry. All you have to do decorating its layers with gads of butter or -- trick -- use a light spray of olive oil instead.

4. Phyllo dough is tissue-thin pastry dough. You might know it ...it is used in many Greek and Middle Eastern dishes. Phyllo dough can be used as a substitute for strudel dough or for other pastry wrappers, for instance, turnovers or spring rolls.
5. Puff Pastry is preferable for pie shells. It is easier. Puff Pastry leaves you working with one sheet --instead of 10 stacked sheets of Phyllo.
6. Puff pastry doesn't dry-out as quickly as Phyllo.
7. Phyllo dough, you --usually-- have to defrost.
8. And, if you do: Phyllo dough takes 24 hours to defrost.
9. Puff pastry sheets are ready to use within 15 minutes.

Coconut Oil

It is excellent to cook with and you can rub it into your hair and lather your skin in it afterward. But despite coconut oil's good reputation, it is not always clear whether or not one should use it because of the trans fat and fatty acid confusion.

Essential fatty acids are good.

Trans fats provide no nutritional value.

Trans fats increase the risk of coronary heart disease by raising levels of "bad" LDL cholesterol and lowering levels of "good" HDL cholesterol. Trans fats occur in small amounts naturally in dairy and meat, but also artificially in a lot of processed foods and some margarines.

Coconut oil has been getting a bad reputation in some circles primarily because of the fats issue and confusion around it caused by past studies on coconut oil used partially hydrogenated coconut oil (not the same thing). The truth is that virgin coconut oil contains zero trans fats and virgin coconut oil is often confused with palm oil.

Fast Facts:
1. Virgin coconut oil is free of trans fat.
2. Coconut oil is 90% saturated fat. Saturated fat is not as evil as previously thought.
3. Coconut oil is heat stable – the best oil to use when cooking at high temperatures, such as frying.
4. Coconut oil is high in lauric acid. Lauric Acid responsible for increasing HDL ("good cholesterol"). So much so, it is more than any other fatty acid, unsaturated or saturated!

5. Lauric Acid is same compound found in mother's' milk that☐transforms into monolaurin, it is responsible for helping to strengthen the immune system.
6. It also increases metabolism, which can improve thyroid activity and cell regeneration.
7. Pure coconut oil is liquid at room temperature, but turns solid below 25°C/77°F.
8. Coconut oil is an excellent alternative to margarine. It taste great. And, all forms, including non-hydrogenated margarine, is man made.

Tips:
- Coconut Oil is sold at most health food stores.
- When selecting which coconut oil is right for you, ensure that you are buying virgin coconut oil that has not been altered -- including having been heated or bleached.
- Look for non-GMO and organic coconut oil.
- If you need to liquefy you coconut oil, simply place your container in a bowl of hot water and stir or leave it at room temperature for an hour.
- Put one container of coconut oil in the fridge for cooking and store another at room temperature for using as a skin product.

What can you do with Coconut Oil?
- Fry vegetables.
- Using as a replacement margarine and/or butter.
- Lotion: use coconut oil on your skin after a bath.
- Use it to shave your legs.
- Condition your hair.
- Eye makeup remover.
- It's great for pets too -- you can add it to your dog's food (1 tablespoon). It is great for their coat and helps them medicinally the same way it does when humans digest it.

Quinoa

This 100% protein grain has been growing in popularity and there is a good reason why. It is light, easy to cook, and mixes well with a variety of foods and flavors because it has not overarching taste of its own. It grows in the high mountain of Peru and in a similar climate in Colorado. Quinoa originates from the Andean region of South America, where people have been farming & eating it 3000 to 4000 years. The Incas saw the crop as sacred and referring to it as "mother of all grains".

Fast Facts:
1. Quinoa is a grain grown primarily for its edible seeds.
2. It is surprisingly related to beets, spinach, and tumbleweeds.
3. Quinoa's grains range in color from white, to red and black.
4. Each grain is coated with a coating that acts as a natural pest deterrent.
5. Quinoa is different from wheat and rice in that it is high in lysine.
6. It is a good source of fiber, phosphorus, magnesium, and iron.
7. Quinoa contains a balanced set of essential amino acids, making it complete protein.
8. It is gluten-free!

Preparation & Cooking
Always rinse your quinoa in a strainer for a few minutes under cold water before cooking with it.

Cooking Quinoa:
1. Bring 1 part quinoa and 2 parts water to boil in a saucepan.
2. Reduce to lowest heat setting, COVER, and simmer for about 15 minutes, until the germ separates from the seed.
3. It's ready when a tiny curl sticks out from the seed.
4. For added flavor in savory dishes, you can cook it in vegetable broth instead of plain water.
5. Once cooked, quinoa has a mild nutty flavor and fluffy texture, similar to couscous.
6. Quinoa can replace couscous or rice in most recipes
7. Just like rice or pasta salads, it is good served cold with veggies/beans and a light dressing.
8. Breakfast quinoa is an irresistible treat that is versatile -- stirring-in maple syrup/nuts/fruit or add to home fries.
9. It is also available in the form of quinoa flakes, which can also be used to make a quinoa breakfast porridge.
10. Use quinoa to make healthy protein balls/bars.
11. Quinoa flour is a great substitute for flour in gluten-free baking.

Swiss Chard

Swiss chard is also known as chard, silverbeet, perpetual spinach, spinach beet, crab beet, and mangold, which is why it confuses everyone and is the reason I am including it in this list.

Swiss Chard is linked to the same species as beets. The word Swiss was used to distinguish it from French spinach varieties in 19th-century seed catalogues however, it roots trace back to Sicily where it is mostly associated with Mediterranean cuisine.

Fast Facts:
1. Its thick stems range from white to yellow to red.
2. It has shiny green ribbed leaves that fall between spinach and kale in terms of toughness and bitterness – so it's actually one of the most versatile greens for cooking.
3. Fresh young chard leaves can be eaten raw.
4. When sautéed, the bitterness of mature leaves will fade and it will taste sweeter than cooked spinach.
5. Swiss Chard is super high in vitamins A, K and C, and is also rich in iron, potassium, dietary fiber and protein.

Tips:
- Always wash before eating, as with any root vegetable.
- Once washed, it should be wrapped in paper towels and refrigerate.
- Only the young leaves will be eaten raw – although some people consume the uncooked mature leaves as well.
- It can be used pretty much anywhere you would use cooked spinach or other thick leafy greens – including casseroles, stir-fries, stuffings, soups, and kinds of pastas.
- The leaves can be seasoned and baked in the oven, just like kale chips.

Tahini

One of the pitfalls of cooking Vegan is recreating interesting flavors. Tahini is a wonderful tool for creating sauces -- dips and salad dressings -- anything with exotic flavors, due to its exquisite flavor which are rich, nutty, earthy and deep.

Fast Facts:
1. Tahini is a paste made of ground sesame seeds, and has a nutty and slightly earthy taste.
2. If the sesame seed husks are removed, it is referred to as *hulled*.
3. Some tahini contains lightly roasted sesame seeds, other types use raw sesame seeds.
4. Tahini comes from ancient Persia and has been around since at least the 13th century.
5. Middle Eastern foods use a lot of tahini.

6. It is sold fresh or dehydrated.
7. Like any natural nut or seed butter, the natural oils may separate after a certain period of time – simply use a spoon to mix it back together before using.

Uses:
- It is common in Middle Eastern recipes including: Hummus – along with chickpeas, lemon juice, and olive oil (the more tahini, the creamier the hummus).
- Baba ganoush – roasted eggplant dip.
- If you've ever eaten a falafel or shawarma wrap, then it may have been served with a thin white sauce of watered-down tahini.
- It is the main ingredient in halva, a sweet dessert made with tahini and sugar.
- It tastes great in salad dressings and makes them thicker/creamier.
- Add a tablespoon to smoothies for an extra protein boost.

Nutritional Yeast

Nutritional Yeast and the purpose for its use beacons back to the reason Vegan cooking aims, in part, to imitate foods we are used to and enjoy eating. Nutritional Yeast add a "cheesy" taste to food which makes it adored by vegans and anyone who cannot for whatever reasons consume dairy. It is not something one commonly sees mainly because it is not used in commercial food products. Knowing about it places you ahead of the curve ball so far as being able to competently suss out where the limits are.

Fast Facts:
1. It is a deactivated yeast and a fungus.
2. It is produced by culturing the yeast with a mixture of sugar cane and beet molasses for a period of 7 days, then harvesting, washing, drying and packaging the yeast.
3. Its flakes are bright yellow in color.
4. It is a complete protein. This meaning it contains an adequate proportion of all nine essential amino acid that we need to function.
5. It is a good source of protein and B vitamins.
6. It is low in fat and sodium and is free of sugar, dairy and gluten.
7. It has a strong nutty-cheesy flavor that can be added to any dish to impart a cheesy taste.

Uses:
- Grind it in a food processor with an equal part of blanched almonds to mimic Parmesan.

- Add a tablespoon or two to risotto, quiches, cannelloni, stuffed mushrooms – anywhere you would normally use Parmesan or other cheese.
- Sprinkle it on popcorn.
- Blend it with nuts to make vegan cheese sauce, and soft or hard cheese.
- Do NOT confuse it with Brewer's Yeast, which is a by-product of the brewing industry.
- Most good health food stores will stock nutritional yeast.

Agar

Agar is a natural congealing agent.

Fast Facts:
1. It is a flavorless gelling agent.
2. It is derived from Gracilaria, a bright red sea vegetable (seaweed).
3. It is also as Agar.
4. It is available flaked, powdered, or in bars.
5. Agar flakes are traditionally produced by cooking and pressing the seaweed and then naturally freeze-drying the residue to form bars which are then powdered or flaked.
6. It is rich in iodine and trace minerals, and has mildly laxative properties.
7. It is used as a growth medium for petri dishes to grow mold and bacteria.
8. It is often used as a gelling agent in food preparation which is why it is included on this list.

Cooking:
Agar helps foods congeal. This is why it can be, and often is, used in place of gelatin. For example, Agar is often used to make jellies, custards and puddings.

One reason it is popular is due its strong gelling properties than other congealing agents. It is fast acting and take about an hour before it sets. That is as good a time estimate as we can provide. Elements like room temperature and humidity can elongate or shorten this calculation. Unlike gelatin, agar can be boiled. It can also be re-melted, if so needed.

Flake and Bar Forms:
We recommend grinding your agar. Most folks use a coffee grinder or food processor and then cook it, stirring it regularly until it dissolves. Because of density variations, flaked and powdered agar needs to be used in different proportions:

- 1 tbsp. of agar flakes = 1 tsp. of agar powder

Alternatively, use substitute powdered agar in equal amounts for recipes that call for unflavored gelatin.

To make a firm gel, is easy. You just add more agars. For a softer gel, add more liquid! It is really that easy.

You should take note various conditions and mixtures affect agar.

Highly acidic or alkaline ingredients affect the gelling ability of agar. Recipes calling for citrus fruits (oranges, lemons, etc.) and strawberries may require higher amounts of agar to set.

Likewise, there are ingredients that break down the gelling ability of the agar that will cause it to not set. **Cooking these fruits beforehand is a good trick of the trade. Example: Mangoes, papaya, pineapple, kiwi fruit, figs and peaches.

Final thoughts

Thinking outside the box: Asian grocery stores offer an array of affordable sauces as well as otherwise hard to find items: rice paper wrappers and dehydrated mushrooms. But this kind of shopping will only come in handy if you have a propensity for Asian food, which let's face it, is really, really good! Otherwise, as one delves more and more into the wonderful world of Vegan cooking, they will begin to drift into new territories. As the comfort level of cooking Vegan develops, so too will the desire try new dishes.

Chapter 6: Smoothies

They can be high in fiber that is bursting with antioxidants, omega 3 fatty acids, Vitamin C, folic acid and phytonutrients but no matter what, they almost always taste good, despite being good for you. Some will fulfill your yearning for fresh seasonal berries ripe under the August sun. During the winter months, one can equally dive into the tastes of summer -- just pick up a bag of frozen fruit and let the fast that your core ingredient is cold as ice act as your ice substitute.

Smoothies are easy on the pocket book. Easy on the taste buds, Easy on a tight schedule. They are fun to drink and offer reprieve from breakfast which so often turns into the most routine meal of the day. Whether one is clinging to a strict Vegan diet or not, Smoothies are a divine way to treat one's self to something special, sweet and so very good.

We are including them here just before our Breakfast chapter. They are an excellent idea for breakfast. In fact, Chapters 6 and 7 should be thought of as independent meal ideas and combined breakfast options. Smoothies are a fast, easy pick me up source of nourishment that are perfect for the start of one's day. They are also surprisingly filling -- sometimes more so than an English Breakfast!

No matter when they are consumed, they quench a sweet tooth yearning which is another aspect to keep in mind when reaching for something not out of hunger alone.

Strawberry Fields Forever Breakfast Smoothie

Bursting with sweet pick-me-up natural fruit flavor, this smoothie brings rich visual pleasure with it, too. Its Safire red tones are complimented by a rich, creamy texture. The oat and strawberry blend is filling and the smoothie itself is incredibly fast and easy to make. Start your morning out with a nourishing field of forever and never feel hungry before noon.

Time: 6 mins
Quantity: 1 serving

Ingredients:
- 1 cup Vegan Milk (coconut; almond milk; soy milk)
- 1/2 cup Rolled Oats
- 1 Banana, broken into chunks
- 14 frozen Strawberries
- 1/2 teaspoon Vanilla Extract
- 1 1/2 teaspoons White Sugar

Method:
1. Find your blender.
2. Combine soy Almond milk, oats, banana and strawberries.
3. Add vanilla and sugar if desired.
4. Blend until smooth.
5. Pour into glasses and serve.
6. Now, get out the door and get on with your day!

***If too thick, add a splash more juice or water. For more sweetness, add extra frozen banana.*

Hudson River View

This is a super smoothie to make on an overcast day when the sky is nothing but a dull indefinable solid gray that is expected to linger and most people are expected to linger under. Hudson River View is purposely created from ingredients that are invigorating to your taste buds and to your whole body.

Time: 6 mins
Quantity: 1 serving

Ingredients:
- 1 Mango - peeled, seeded, and cut into chunks
- 1 Banana, peeled and chopped
- 1 inch finely chopped fresh Ginger
- 1 cup Orange Juice
- 1 cup Vanilla Non-fat Yogurt

Method:
1. Get out your blender.
2. In a bowl add the ginger, mango, banana, orange juice, and yoghurt.
3. Mix thoroughly.
4. Pour everything from the bowl into the blender.
5. Blend until smooth.
6. Serve in clear glasses, and drink with a bendy straw!

***If too thick, add a splash more juice or water. For more sweetness, add extra frozen banana.*

Oh, Bahama Mama

Imagine your mother telling you to eat your greens. Well, Bahama Mama is inspired by what your mother would want you to eat and what you might prefer to eat. Believe it or not, the culmination of both makes a screamingly savvy smoothie that is sublime. The core ingredients are Kale and Banana -- go figure. It works! Maybe you can have your cake and eat it, too?

Time: 4 mins
Quantity: 1 serving

Ingredients:
- 1 Banana
- 2 cups chopped Kale
- 1/2 cup Vegan Milk (coconut; almond milk; soymilk)
- 1 tablespoon Flaxseeds
- 1 teaspoon Maple Syrup

Method:
1. Get out your blender.
2. Place the banana, kale, 1 cup vegan milk (coconut; almond milk; soy milk) flaxseeds, and maple syrup into a bowl.
3. Mix all the ingredients.
4. Transfer to blender.
5. Cover, and puree until smooth.
6. Serve over ice.

***If too thick, add a splash more juice or water. For more sweetness, add extra frozen banana.

Tupelo Grove

Elvis Presley was widely known for his love for chocolate and bananas. Pop them in your blender in the morning to your favorite Elvis tune and shake rattle and roll through your week with an extra energy boost in your every step because this puppy is loaded with good stuff. Peanut butter provides protein and bananas help the body focus and stay on track.

Time: 4 mins
Quantity: 1 serving

Ingredients:
- 2 Bananas, broken into chunks
- 1/2 cup Peanut Butter
- 2 tablespoons Honey
- 2 cups ice cubes
- 2 cups Vegan Milk (coconut; almond milk; soymilk)

Method:
1. Find your blender.
2. Place bananas, peanut butter, honey, and ice cubes in a bowl.
3. Pour them into blender after giving them a slow stir by hand.
4. Blend until smooth, about 30 seconds.
5. Empty into a large glass and rock the day away!

***If too thick, add a splash more juice or water. For more sweetness, add extra frozen banana.*

Georgia On My Mind

Summer in Georgia means peaches -- lots of them! Put in peach in your smoothie. They are smooth, nurturing, nutritious and will remind you to appreciate the little things in life.

Time: 4 mins
Quantity: 1 serving

Ingredients:
- 2 fresh Peaches, peeled
- ½ Banana
- 1 cup Vegan Milk (coconut, almond, or soymilk)
- 1 cup ice cubes
- 1 tablespoon Agave Nectar or Maple Syrup

Method:
1. After washing fresh peaches, slice and remove the pits.
2. Add peach wedges to a bowl.
3. Peel banana.
4. Slice into small bits.
5. Pour fruit into blender.
6. Add ice, vegan milk choice, and sweetener.
7. Using a blender, blend all ingredients until smooth.
8. Serve and enjoy immediately.

***If too thick, add a splash more juice or water. For more sweetness, add extra frozen banana.

Jealous Julius

Jealous Julius is like drinking the sweet nectar from an orange that has been freshly plucked from a tree -- which would make a lot of folks jealous! Hence, the name. The smoothie is an excellent and exciting way to invigorate one's day. A Jealous Julious can complement the morning to spice things up. Alternatively, it is a great option on a hot afternoon day in the summer.

Time: 3 mins
Quantity: 1 serving

Ingredients:
- 1 cup Orange Juice (fresh is best)
- 1 cup ice cubes
- ½ Banana
- 3 tablespoons Vegan Vanilla Protein Powder

Method:
1. Get your frozen juice out of the freezer or fresh juice out of the fridge.
2. Add to a bowl.
3. Add banana, mix in protein powder.
4. Pour all ingredients to a blender and blend on high until smooth.
5. Pour into two serving glasses and enjoy.

***If too thick, add a splash more juice or water. For more sweetness, add extra frozen banana.*

Boyz N Berry

If you are looking for something high in fiber that is bursting with antioxidants, omega 3 fatty acids, Vitamin C, folic acid and phytonutrients among other things, look no further! Seriously --- *this* is your smoothie! Maybe you are leaping on the smoothies wagon to help quell your sweet tooth that went crazy over the weekend. Whatever the reason, Berry, Berry is very healthy and sweet as a fresh summer's kiss.

Time: 6 mins
Quantity: 1 serving

Ingredients:
- 1 cup frozen Berries
- 1 cup organic Spinach or Kale
- ½ cup Banana, previously peeled, sliced and frozen
- 1 tablespoon Flaxseeds meal
- 1 cup Pomegranate Juice
- 1 tablespoon silken Tofu

Method:
1. Get you frozen berries out of the freezer.
2. Add berries to a bowl.
3. Add flaxseed, juice, tofu – hand mix.
4. Pour all ingredients to a blender and blend on high until smooth.
5. Pour into two serving glasses and enjoy.

**If too thick, add a splash more juice or water. For more sweetness, add extra frozen banana.*

Blueberry Hill

There are two things that grow in Maine. Mix them together and a new world is born. Blueberries and fresh maple syrup are a killer good combination. Sweet, nature, pure, nutritious and perfect in a smoothie.

Time: 6 mins
Quantity: 1 serving

Ingredients:
- ½ Almond milk
- 1 scoop Vanilla Protein Powder
- ½ cup frozen Blueberries
- ¼ - ½ teaspoon Maple Extract
- ¼ teaspoon Vanilla Extract
- 2 teaspoons Flaxseeds meal
- Maple syrup
- 10 – 15 ice cubes + ¼ cup water

Method:
1. Add your blueberries, flaxseeds, extracts, and maple syrup together in a bowl.
2. Mix them together.
3. Slowly stir in the almond milk.
4. Pour all the ingredients in a blender and mix until well combined.

***If too thick, add a splash more juice or water. For more sweetness, add extra frozen banana.

Sherry Lady

Sherry baby is inspired from a 1950's recipe that has been totally converted to taste explosively excellent but be far healthier than the inspiration of its genesis. The nectarine and cherry combination are enhanced by lime. When you put this to your lips, you will witness something that is unlike any other smoothie you have ever tried!

Time: 4 mins
Quantity: 1 serving

Ingredients:

- 1 ripe Nectarine or Peach, sliced
- 1 heaping cup fresh or frozen Cherries (add less if using frozen)
- ¾ cup Almond milk (or sub water or other Vegan milk)
- 1 – 2 Limes, juiced
- Handful of ice
- 6 Spinach leaves

Method:

1. Slice and pit your nectarine.
2. Make sure cherries are pitted and halved.
3. Add both to a bowl. Mix.
4. Pour into a blender.
5. Add some of your ice.
6. Slowly pour in Almond milk.
7. Pulse the blender until the ice cubes are small enough to switch to full blend.
8. Pour into glass and enjoy!

***If too thick, add a splash more juice or water. For more sweetness, add extra frozen banana*

Pale Mail

Odd as it may seem, smoothies go further than providing a daily dose of fruit. This one asks for kale and blueberries which do not seem at the onset like regular bedfellows. Toss a banana in there, and three is never a crowd. Pale Mail will thrill you by surprising you with what's inside!

Time: 4 mins
Quantity: 1 serving

Ingredients:

- 1 medium ripe Banana
- ½ cup frozen mixed Berries
- 1 heaping tablespoon Flaxseeds
- 2 cups frozen or fresh Kale, any kind
- 2/3 cup 100% Pomegranate Juice
- ¾ - 1 ½ cups filtered water

Method:

1. Peel banana and dice into bite sized pieces.
2. Place banana in bowl along with berries. Mix.
3. Pour pomegranate juice and add kale and flaxseeds to blender – blend (high).
4. Pour into glass and enjoy!

***If too thick, add a splash more juice or water. For more sweetness, add extra frozen banana.*

Chapter 7: Breakfast

It has been said so many times. Breakfast is the most important meal of the day. And -- it is. We decided to draw from traditional recipes. Here, you will find how to make an Egg McMuffin! To balance the act, we added many fruit and grain based recipes that will delight you for many reasons. One being, they are quicker than quick to toss together. Vegan dishes can take some time and thought before eating. Sometimes, that is not enough. Literally, there are a few recipes in here that can be put together in a matter of minutes. The only caveat is that you are sure to buy all the necessary -- anticipated -- ingredients. All of which we have included in the extensive list in an earlier chapter.

As mentioned earlier, ingredients like quinoa are often utilized in Vegan cooking. This is true about breakfast. This 100% protein grain has been growing in popularity and there is a good reason why. It is light, easy to cook, and mixes well with a variety of foods and flavors because it has not overarching taste of its own. It grows in the high mountain of Peru and in a similar climate in Colorado. Quinoa originates from the Andean region of South America, where people have been farming & eating it 3000 to 4000 years. The Incas saw the crop as sacred and referring to it as "mother of all grains".

We also mention Nutritional Yeast and that the purpose for its use beacons back to the reason Vegan cooking aims, in part, to imitate foods we are used to and enjoy eating. Nutritional Yeast add a "cheesy" taste to food which makes it adored by vegans and anyone who cannot for whatever reasons consume dairy. It is not something one commonly sees mainly because it is not used in commercial food products. Knowing about it places you ahead of the curve ball so far as being able to competently suss out where the limits are. Of course, along with all this we will remind you again that in the chapter preceding this one -- *smoothies* -- can be used as an extension of the recipes that follow. Cooking is an art! Mix, match, and be the master of your universe!

Vegan Egg McMuffins

You do not have to cut out every part of what makes food fun! The exciting think about Vegan cooking is its propensity toward imitation. That means, you can have your cake and eat it, too. The cake in this case is an Egg McMuffin. Bon appetit!

Time: 12 mins
Quantity: 1 serving

Ingredients:
- 1 block firm Tofu
- Vegetable oil
- ¼ teaspoon Turmeric powder
- Garlic powder
- Black pepper
- 1 slice Vegan Canadian Bacon
- 1 Vegan English Muffin
- 1 slice Vegan Cheddar Cheese
- Vegan Margarine spread

Method:
1. Slice 1/3 of the tofu unto a square.
2. Sprinkle tofu with turmeric powder.
3. Season with garlic powder and black pepper.
4. Heat 1 teaspoon oil in a frying pan and cook the tofu.
5. Add Vegan Canadian bacon, so that they are browned on both sides.
6. Meanwhile, toast the English muffin and butter with vegan margarine.
7. Assemble the sandwich using the cheese, tofu and vegan bacon.

White Sandy Beach Delight

We do not want to imprison you with egg based recipes so we came up with some fruit based ideas. Bursting fruit flavors keep the body and mind light whereas other breakfast options can weigh a person down. Try this recipe on a cold winter day to beat the blues away.

Time: 10 mins
Quantity: 1 serving

Ingredients:
- 1 tablespoon dried Coconut
- ¼ cup fresh Pineapple
- 1/3 cup blend of Oatmeal
- 1.3 cup Quinoa flakes
- ¾ cup water of Soymilk

Method:
1. Toast the coconut in a frying pan or oven until golden. Watch it carefully so that it doesn't burn!
2. In the meantime, place the oatmeal & quinoa in a microwave-safe bowl with the water or soymilk. Cook on high for 1.5 minutes. Alternatively, you can cook it in a saucepan for a few minutes on the stove.
3. Top with the fresh pineapple and toasted coconut. Enjoy!

Protein Dream

This recipe assures you. Knowing you are getting the protein you need and doing it in a fun way makes protein a dream! Add some oats and honey, both are a good source of energy that will keep you going throughout the day.

Time: 10 mins
Quantity: 1 serving

Ingredients:
- 1 bottle Vanilla Protein
- ½ cup Rolled Oats
- 1 tablespoon Honey
- Raspberries
- Blackberries
- ½ Banana
- Toasted Almonds, chopped
- Raw Chocolate, chopped
- Toasted Coconut

Method:
1. In a bowl, mix protein powder, oats, almonds and coconut.
2. Slice banana into bite sized pieces.
3. In another bowl, add fruit varieties in any order.
4. Pour dry mix over the fruit and stir.
5. Top with raw chocolate.

Don't Cha Know I'm On The Go?

On the days you wake up (late) and have no time whatsoever for breakfast, this is what you turn to. It takes two minutes to make the first few times you go through the steps and less time than that one you allow it into your routine, which is wise. It will save you when the day explodes into chaos and you are still walking around half asleep.

Time: 2 mins
Quantity: 1 serving

Ingredients:
- 1 bottle Vanilla Protein
- 4 tablespoons Chia seeds
- Fresh Raspberries
- Granola
- Honey

Method:
1. Combine ingredients, mixing chia seeds and protein powder first.
2. Add raspberries and granola.
3. Drizzle with honey.

Dream Boat Fruit Blend

When there is time for sleeping in and celebrating (and elongating) the morning hours, this is a fun breakfast that is beautiful, playful, fancy and healthy at the same time. How many things in life can you say that about?

Time: 10 mins
Quantity: 1 serving

Ingredients:
- 1 bottle Chocolate Protein
- 2 Bananas
- ¼ cup Almond butter
- Blueberries
- Dark chocolate, chopped
- White chia
- Tangerine sections

Method:
1. Combine ingredients; Mix chia and protein powder first.
2. Stir in the almond butter
3. Chop banana into bite sized pieces
4. Add blueberries, chocolate, and tangerine sections.
5. Devour and enjoy!

Mood Beams and Marigolds With Coffee

We wanted to include a few different protein recipes to show off that there are many directions flavor wise one can go in and we want to emphasize the importance of getting enough protein in one's diet. From time to time Vegan cooking can go badly when a balance of nutrition is not reached. We have your back!

Time: 5 mins
Quantity: 1 serving

Ingredients:
- 1 bottle Coffee Protein
- 4 tablespoons Chia seeds
- Cherries
- Almond silvers

Method:
1. Combine ingredients, mixing chia seeds and protein powder first.
2. Add cherries.
3. Top with almond silvers.

Breakfast Boats

These are fun for kids and adults alike and put an overlooked fruit to use. Papaya is not utilized often enough because folks are not sure what to do with them. At least, in western culture this has been true for a long time despite that they are available in most grocery stores.

Time: 12 mins
Quantity: 2 serving

Ingredients:

- 1 papaya
- 2 single Greek Yogurt alternative
- Assorted fruits
- Chia seeds
- Flaxseeds
- Honey

Method:

1. Cut the papaya in half lengthwise.
2. Scoop out the black seeds and discard.
3. Fill each papaya half with one container of yogurt.
4. Top with fruit of your choice.
5. Sprinkle on seeds and drizzle with honey.

Mushroom Caps

This is traditional but not very often seen as a breakfast option. Mushroom caps are a glorious way to start the day. They are savory, nutritious, delicious and easy to make. They are also a good easy way to escape standard early morning meals.

Time: 25 mins
Quantity: 3 servings

Ingredients:
- 8 baby Portobello mushrooms or 2 large ones
- 4 tablespoons Olive oil
- 1 tablespoon Olive oil
- 1 Onion, chopped
- 1 clove Garlic, minced
- ¼ cup Walnuts, chopped
- ½ cup Spinach, chopped and tightly packed
- ½ teaspoon dried Sage
- ½ teaspoon dried Thyme
- 1 tablespoon nutritional Yeast
- 1 cup Vegan breadcrumbs
- 1/8 cup Vegetable broth
- Salt and pepper, to taste
- 1 Bell Pepper
- 4 tablespoons Olive oil

Method (Roasted Pepper):
1. Preheat oven to 350 degrees.
2. Cut the pepper in two, and remove the stem. Scrape-out all seeds and all the stringy white flesh.
3. Place face-down onto a baking sheet and roast until the skin is charred.
4. Remove from oven and let cool.
5. Peel the skin.
6. Blend with olive oil in a food processor, season with salt and pepper as needed, set aside.

Method (Mushrooms):
1. Preheat oven to 350 degrees.

2. Wash and dry the mushrooms. Remove the caps and gently scrape-out the gills.
3. In a shallow dish, mix 4 tablespoons olive oil and tamari (optional). Add the mushrooms and spoon the mixture onto the mushrooms.
4. Heat 1 tablespoon of olive oil over medium heat and sauté the onion and garlic until onions are translucent.
5. Add the walnuts, spinach, sage, and thyme. Cook for a few minutes until spinach has wilted.
6. Remove from heat and stir in the nutritional yeast, breadcrumbs, and vegetable broth. Season with salt and pepper to taste. Set aside.
7. Place mushrooms on baking sheet.
8. Bake for 15 minutes.
9. Remove the mushrooms from the oven.
10. Add the filling to each mushroom cap, pressing it tightly together.
11. Return to oven for a few minutes.
12. Serve with roasted red pepper.

Chapter 8: Dressings and Sauces

Vegan food is all encompassing! Yes -- you even have to think about dressing and sauces. Many of these items are milk based. But that does not mean you have to go without them. You can easily make Vegan sauces and dressings yourself. They are really simple, straightforward and require little time and effort. Once made, you will find they can be used in a variety of ways that are not listed here. For example, some of the dressings we have included will compliment any number of salads. Without a doubt, you will find ways to love and enjoy all of these!

As we mentioned in an earlier chapter, one of the pitfalls of cooking Vegan is recreating interesting flavors. Tahini is a wonderful tool for creating sauces -- dips and salad dressings etc.. due to its exquisite flavors which are rich and deep.

Mom's Cream Cheese

For many of you, cream cheese is a taste that was first experienced during childhood. The memories that flood back when biting into this creamy dream are hard to conjure up without it which is why we do not want you do go on without it!

Time: 12 mins
Quantity: 2-3 servings

Ingredients:
- 1/4 cup Coconut oil, melted
- 1 tablespoon Olive oil
- 3 cups cooked Navy beans
- 2 teaspoons Onion powder
- 2 tablespoons fresh Lemon juice
- 2 teaspoons cider vinegar
- 2 tablespoons refined coconut oil
- 2 large yellow onions, finely diced
- Salt and ground black pepper to taste
- Green onions - thinly sliced

Method:
1. Place coconut oil, olive oil, beans, onion powder, lemon juice, cider vinegar, and salt in a food processor.
2. Blend until thick and smooth.
3. Transfer to a large bowl and chill, covered, until cold.
4. Melt oil in a large skillet over medium-high heat.
5. Cook onions with a pinch of salt and a few dashes pepper, stirring frequently, 3 minutes.
6. Reduce heat to low and cook, stirring occasionally, until onions are very soft, sweet, and amber brown.
7. Transfer to a bowl and cool completely.
8. Fold caramelized onions into cream cheese.
9. Season with salt and pepper.
10. Top with green onions.

Super Simple Hummus

Super Simple Hummus is just that -- it is crazy easy to make. It is high in protein and goes on just about anything you want it to. It's good, versatile stuff and we want to make sure you have a reliable recipe on hand because it can be used in so many different dishes.

Time: 12 mins
Quantity: 3 servings

Ingredients:
- 1 can chickpeas washed and drained
- ½ lemon, juiced
- 1 clove garlic, minced
- 2 or 3 heaping tablespoons tahini
- 3 tablespoons olive oil
- 3 tablespoons water, plus more if needed
- ½ teaspoon cumin
- Salt and pepper, to taste
- Paprika

Method:
1. Put everything in a food processor.
2. Blend until smooth.
3. Add additional water if needed.
4. Sprinkle with paprika, and drizzle with additional olive oil before serving.

Guacamole

Slather it on a chip or a sandwich or a finger! Anything with avocado divine --not to mention healthy. This recipe hides broccoli inside the smooth guacamole, creating it tasty crunch and explosion of vitamins and minerals.

Time: 9 mins
Quantity: 2-3 servings

Ingredients:
- 2 ripe avocados, diced
- ¾ cup raw broccoli pieces, finely chopped
- 1 tomato, diced
- ¼ cup red onion, minced
- 1 clove garlic, minced
- 1 tablespoon lemon juice
- Fresh cilantro, chopped
- Salt

Method:
1. Set aside the avocados.
2. Mix all other ingredients.
3. Add the avocados – by gently fold them in so that there are still some chunks.
4. Seasons with salt and pepper.

Mango Black Bean Dip

Black beans are packed with protein. They can be on the dry side but put a mango next to them and watch this match made in heaven seduce you and your friend's taste buds.

Time: 12 mins
Quantity: 2-3 servings

Ingredients:
- 1 can black beans
- 1 red onion, chopped
- 4 roma tomatoes, chopped
- 1 red pepper, chopped
- 375g canned corn kernels, drained
- 1/3 cup fresh cilantro, roughly chopped
- 2 avocados, peeled and diced
- 1 mango, peeled and diced
- 150g rocket leaves

Ingredient (Dressing):
- 1 clove garlic, minced
- 1 small red chili, finely chopped (or ½ teaspoon of crushed red chili pepper)
- 2 tablespoon lime juice
- ¼ cup olive oil

Method (Dip):
1. If not canned, soak the beans in cold water overnight.
2. Place beans into a large heavy-bottomed pan.
3. Cover with water and bring to boil.
4. Reduce the heat and simmer until tender.
5. Drain and cool slightly.
6. Place all dressing ingredients in a large bowl and whisk.
7. Place beans, onions, tomatoes, pepper, corn, cilantro, avocado, mando in a bowl.
8. Mix together.

Bread Spread

Again, we are keeping it simple. We want cooking vegan to be fun and blind you from knowing you are adhering to any kind of diet. This Bread Spread is loaded with protein and will knock your socks off with its smooth and creamy texture that complements more than one type of bread.

Time: 15 mins
Quantity: 5-6 servings

Ingredients:
- 1.5 cups cashews
- ¼ cup nutritional yeast
- 1 clove garlic
- 3 cups rocket leaves
- ¼ cup extra virgin olive oil
- 2 tablespoon lemon juice
- Salt and pepper
- Crushed red chili pepper

Method:
1. In a food processor, add cashews, nutritional yeast and garlic.
2. Pulse gently, so the ingredients are mixed but the cashews are still chunky.
3. Empty into medium-sized bowl and set aside.
4. In the food processor, add the olive oil and lemon juice first, then the rocket. Pulse to blend well.
5. Mix rocket mixture into cashew mixture, and season with salt, pepper, and crushed red chili pepper.
6. Serve on crackers or bread.

Lemon Tahini Dressing

Whether you are a seasoned tahini user or new to the game, your will love the variety of dressings we have listed here for you to splash on your beds of lettuce. This stuff with bring even the most dull salads to life! Tahini is a paste made of ground sesame seeds, and has a nutty and slightly earthy taste.

Time: 6 mins
Quantity: 2-3 servings

Ingredients:
- ½ cup tahini
- Juice of 1 large lemon
- ¼ teaspoon salt
- 3-6 tablespoons warm water

Sweet and Sour Tahini Dressing

Tahini is a paste made of ground sesame seeds, and has a nutty and slightly earthy taste. It is also a versatile product. It can go in many directions with its flavor and given its texture which is what you will discover when you make Sweet and Sour Tahini.

Time: 8 mins
Quantity: 2-3 servings

Ingredients:
- 3 tablespoons tahini
- 2 tablespoons extra virgin olive oil
- 3 tablespoons freshly squeezed lemon juice
- 2 garlic cloves, crushed
- ½ teaspoons brown rice syrup
- ½ teaspoons ground cumin
- ¼ teaspoons cinnamon
- ¼ teaspoons salt

Method (Dressing):
1. Add the garlic, tahini, olive oil, lemon juice, brown rice syrup, cinnamon, cumin and salt into a small blender.
2. Mix until smooth (so easy!).

Mustard Vinaigrette Dressing

Mustard Vinaigrette Dressing harkens back to flavors and cravings many of us are used to having. For this book, we wanted to pack in in what is familiar that created comfort. This is one of those recipes you can use on a lot of different dishes that will evoke a lot of memories while creating new ones.

Time: 6 mins
Quantity: 2-3 servings

Ingredients:
- ½ cup olive oil
- 5 tablespoons apple cider vinegar
- 1 teaspoon sweet mustard
- Salt and pepper, to taste

Method:
1. Mix olive oil and sweet mustard together – whip.
2. Pour in apple cider vinegar.
3. Drizzle over whatever food you desire.

Able Mable Dressing

If you are craving something sweet, Able Mable Dressing is the answer. Its maple base is sweet as honey. Toss in the sesame oil and you have a full-on flavor festival going on!

Time: 5 mins
Quantity: 2-3 servings

Ingredients:
- 1 tablespoon real maple syrup
- 1 tablespoon extra virgin olive oil
- 1 tablespoon sesame oil
- 2 tablespoons apple cider vinegar
- 1 teaspoon white sesame seeds
- 1 tablespoon soy sauce
- Pepper, to taste
- 1 garlic clove, crushed and then minced

Method:
1. Add the syrup, olive oil, lemon juice, soy sauce, pepper, vinegar, sesame, and garlic into a small blender.
2. Mix until smooth.

Dijon Dressing

What would life be without Dijon dressing? Again, when looking for recipes to add to our book, we wanted to include those that are most likely to be familiar to you...except they are made in ways you have never before tried!

Time: 6 mins
Quantity: 2-3 servings

Ingredients:
- 1/3 cup extra virgin olive oil
- 1 tablespoon vegan mayonnaise
- 1 tablespoon Dijon mustard
- 1 garlic clove, minced
- 1 teaspoon maple syrup
- ¼ teaspoon salt

Method:
1. Add the garlic, maple syrup, salt and Dijon into a small blender.
2. Mix until smooth.

Chapter 9: Salads

Salads are an obvious go-to because Veganism is a plant-based diet. While this can like an uneventful setup, it can, in fact, be a glorious one. Everything that makes eating eventful starts with imagination. For many of us, salads spent years consisting of unevenly sliced cucumbers, damp leaves of iceberg lettuce, ranch dressing and, if lucky, a wedge of a tasteless tomato. Boy, things have changed -- and for the better!

The number of new diets hitting the markets has changed the face of standard food presentation. The Vegan movement has done this in a couple of ways. It has invented new ways to imitate the good ole days at the same time it has brought never before thought of foods into the fold. The salads we include in this book demonstrate a little of both. Most any of these are easily be pared with the dressings included in the previous chapter. That is only if you want to mix it up. A lot of our salads have a special dressing --suggestion -- that complements the various flavors by enhancing them.

Along with tasting great, salads are excellent for promoting and sustaining good health. They are packed with antioxidants that cleanse and nourish one's body at the same time. You cannot go wrong when choosing what salad to have and you cannot really have too much of such a good thing, so make your salad big, broad and bulging!

Autumn Song

The joys of Autumn and the foods that seasonal come with it burst through this joyful salad that is rich in flavor and healthy ingredients. Many end of the season mixes mark the changing of the year, in this case from summer to autumn. The air is chillier. The night's darkness blankets over one a little longer. The leaves begin to change. What is left in the garden marks the nearness of the last harvest. A hodge podge of treats that can come together like a song.

Time: 15 mins
Quantity: 3 servings

Ingredients:
- 1 medium butternut squash
- Salt and pepper, to taste
- 1 large pear
- 5 oz arugula
- ¾ cup pomegranate seeds
- ¾ cup roughly chopped walnuts

Ingredients (Dressing):
- 1 tablespoon real maple syrup
- 1 tablespoon extra virgin olive oil
- 1 tablespoon sesame oil
- 2 tablespoons apple cider vinegar
- 1 teaspoon white sesame seeds
- 1 teaspoon soy sauce
- Pepper, to taste
- 1 garlic clove, crushed and then minced

Method (Salad):
1. Preheat the oven to 400 degrees.
2. Line a baking sheet with parchment paper and lay out the butternut squash noodles.
3. Coat lightly with cooking spray.
4. While the squash cooks, combine all of the ingredients for the vinaigrette and set aside.
5. Add the pear to a large mixing bowl with the arugula and walnuts.
6. Add butternut squash to a bowl, coat with the dressing and toss thoroughly.
7. Serve immediately.

Silk Road Salad

In ancient times the most active trading routes was that of the Silk Road. This recipe is inspired by the vast variety of grains, nuts, and dried fruits that could be found there.

Time: 15 mins
Quantity: 3 servings

Ingredients:
- 1 cup cooked wild rice
- 1 cup cooked red quinoa
- 1 cup cooked farro
- ¼ toasted chopped walnuts
- ¼ cup toasted chopped pecans
- ¼ cup pistachios, roughly chopped
- ¼ cup dried cranberries
- ¼ cup dried apricots, finely chopped
- ¼ cup golden raisins
- ¼ cup brown raisins
- ¼ cup fresh pomegranate seeds, plus extra for garnish
- 4 scallions, thinly sliced, green and white parts
- ¼ large red onion, minced
- Celery finely diced

Ingredients (Dressing):
- ½ cup olive oil
- 5 tablespoons apple cider vinegar
- 1 teaspoon sweet mustard
- Salt and pepper, to taste

Method (Salad):
1. Mix the salad ingredients together in a large bowl.
2. Pour the dressing ingredients together and add enough to the salad.
3. Cover and refrigerate.
4. Coat with pomegranate seeds before serving.

Sweet Potatoes On The Bay

A lot of California inspired dishes are made from a culmination of ingredients. This salad is no exception. Dried fruits, avocado and kale demonstrate the rich variety of culinary possibility the Sunshine State has on offer. This salad complements a wide range of meals and alone can be considered a meal itself.

Time: 15 mins
Quantity: 3 servings

Ingredients:
- 2 medium sweet potatoes, peeled and diced
- 2 teaspoons + 1 teaspoon olive oil
- ¾ teaspoon salt
- ¼ teaspoon black pepper
- 1 bunch of curly kale, washed
- Juice of ½ a large lemon
- 1 can garbanzo beans
- 1 large avocado, pitted and diced
- 1/3 cup dried cranberries
- 1/3 cup chopped almonds
- ¼ chopped red onion

Ingredients (Dressing):
- 3 tablespoons tahini
- 2 tablespoons extra virgin olive oil
- 3 tablespoons freshly squeezed lemon juice
- 2 garlic cloves, crushed
- ½ teaspoon brown rice syrup
- ½ teaspoon ground cumin
- ¼ teaspoon cinnamon
- ¼ teaspoon salt

Method (Salad):
1. Preheat oven to 375 degrees.
2. On a large sheet pan, toss together the diced sweet potato with 2 teaspoons olive oil, 1/2 teaspoon salt and 1/4 teaspoon of pepper.
3. Bake sweet potatoes until fork tender, 35-40 minutes.

4. Prepare the kale while the sweet potatoes are baking.
5. Add the chopped kale to a large bowl with 1 tbsp olive oil, juice of ½ a large lemon and a heaping ¼ tsp salt.
6. Massage the kale and make sure everything is mixed together.
7. Set kale aside until sweet potatoes are finished baking.
8. Make the dressing by adding all ingredients to a bowl and whisking until a creamy dressing is formed. Add the water slowly until desired consistency is reached.
9. Add the kale mixture to separate bowls and evenly top with remaining ingredients and dress.

Big Sky Salad

Big Sky Salad offers up a fresh assortment of mouthwatering flavors. At its core is sweet potato which is one of the most amazingly nourishing and filling foods that cannot be consumed enough. It is packed with properties that balance hormones which means it can help in maintaining a balanced mind while nourishing one's spirit.

Time: 45 mins
Quantity: 3 servings

Ingredients:
- 1 medium sweet potato
- 1 courgette
- 1 carrot
- 1 red pepper
- 1 red onion
- 1 tablespoon olive oil
- 1 tablespoon dried mixed herbs
- ½ teaspoon salt
- Freshly ground black pepper, to taste
- 1 cup quinoa
- 1 cup kale
- ½ cup frozen peas
- 4 cups water
- ½ teaspoon vegetable stock powder

Ingredients (Dressing):
- 3 tablespoons tahini
- 2 tablespoons extra virgin olive oil
- 3 tablespoons freshly squeezed lemon juice
- 2 garlic cloves, crushed
- ½ teaspoon brown rice syrup
- ½ teaspoon ground cumin
- ¼ teaspoon cinnamon
- ¼ teaspoon salt

Method (Salad):

1. Preheat oven to 325 degrees.
2. Peel and chop the sweet potato and carrot.
3. Chop the sweet potato, carrot, red pepper, and courgette into rough chunks/cubes, and slice the onion into narrow wedge shapes.
4. Add them into a large dish.
5. Coat with olive oil, dried mixed herbs, salt and pepper.
6. Stir them all together, and add them into the oven to cook for about 20-25 minutes.

Method (Quinoa):

1. Add the water and vegetable stock into a pan on medium heat.
2. Bring the water to a boil and add in the quinoa.
3. Cook for 10 minutes.
4. Add in the kale and peas.
5. Remove from the heat, drain.
6. Transfer to a large mixing bowl.
7. Mix everything together, divide onto plates (add dressing).
8. Method (Dressing):
9. Add the garlic, tahini, olive oil, lemon juice, brown rice syrup, cinnamon, cumin, and salt into a small blender.
10. Mix until smooth.

Santa Fe Vegan Salad

Cultures collide! Mexican and American foods have been borrowing from one another for well over a hundred years. Taking from some of those results, this vegan salad offers a welcome change of pace that breaks from the standard use of greens as the center piece. Black beans abound and so does the spice rack. This salad really brings an explosion of flavor variety that is outside the scope of many vegan dishes. When you want to create something that looks and tastes a new, Santa Fe should be your first stop.

Time: 45 mins
Quantity: 3 servings

Ingredients:

- 1 15 oz can black beans
- 2 teaspoons chili powder
- ½ teaspoon salt
- ½ teaspoon garlic powder
- ½ teaspoon paprika powder
- 1 teaspoon cumin
- ¼ cup water
- 1 15 oz can chickpeas
- 1 teaspoon chili powder
- 1 teaspoon cumin
- ½ teaspoon salt
- ¼ teaspoon cinnamon
- 1 head green leaf lettuce
- 1-2 chopped tomatoes
- 1 red bell pepper, chopped
- 1 avocado, chopped
- 1 can fresh corn kernels

Method:

1. Preheat oven to 400 degrees F.
2. Toss chickpeas with the chili powder, cumin, salt and cinnamon.
3. Place chickpeas on a baking sheet in one even layer and bake for 20-30 minutes, shaking them around 1/2 way through.
4. Toss the black beans with all the spices and warm in a pan over medium heat with 1/4 cup water.

5. Stir occasionally until warmed through, about 5-6 minutes.
6. To assemble the salad, toss the lettuce, tomatoes, peppers, avocado and corn in a large bowl. Plate the lettuce mixture on each individual plate or bowl. Add the black beans to the individual servings and top with the crunchy roasted chickpeas.
7. Drizzle with the Dijon dressing.

Chelsey Morning

This salad comes straight from the Big Apple where staying began takes a lot of groovy effort and sass. It is not easy to keep a candle lit in the city that never sleeps. Chelsey Morning is created from a combination of ingredients that keep a person on their toes. Energy, purity, determination are the hoped for effects that manifest after eating this sweet blast of greens.

Time: 20 mins
Quantity: 3 servings

Ingredients:
- 14 oz extra firm tofu
- 1 tablespoon sesame oil
- 2 cucumbers, sliced
- 3 large carrots, diced
- 3 green onions, chopped
- ½ cup cilantro
- ½ bell pepper, sliced
- ½ green chili pepper, sliced
- 1 cup roasted almond slivers

Ingredients (Dressing):
- ½ cup tahini
- Juice of 1 large lemon
- ¼ teaspoon salt
- 3-6 tablespoons warm water

Method (Salad):
1. Add 1 tablespoon of sesame oil to pan over medium heat.
2. Cut the tofu into small cubes and add them to the pan.
3. Brown the tofu for about 10 minutes, turning occasionally.
4. Slice the cucumber into a colander.
5. Mix the dressing ingredients in a food processor until smooth.
6. Combine everything in a large mixing bowl.
7. Pour the dressing over and toss to coat.

Chapter 10: Side Dishes

The following Vegan side dish recipes are super easy to make and taste incredibly great. As with all the recipes throughout this book, they are not far outside cuisine standards you are used to eating. Stuffed peppers are excellent as complementary side dishes with anything from salad to pizza. You just cut them into servings that reflect the amount of expected guests. Alternatively, one can make these ruby gems as an entree. A whole one on it's own is quite filling. The peppers are high in fiber and many folks find them helpful to aid in losing weight. They are high in vitamins E and B6.

Couscous is a versatile side dish. Couscous is useful to get acquainted with if you have not been introduced. It not only complements an expansive array of entrees, it can easily be converted into one by adding a few vegetables. Also in this chapter you will find at least one recipe that calls for *Aquafaba*. We mention this in an early chapter: Aquafaba is the liquid from cooked chickpeas which are commonly sold at all grocery stores.

Ruby Red Bells Peppers

Time: 25mins
Quantity: 2-3 servings

Ingredients:
- 1 lb tempeh
- 2 cups cooked rice
- 1 medium onion, diced
- 1 clove garlic, minced
- 2 tablespoons vegetable oil
- 1/2 cup chopped tomatoes, drained
- 1/2 teaspoon thyme
- 1/2 teaspoon salt
- 1/8 teaspoon pepper
- 1/4 cup chopped parsley
- 1/4 cup breadcrumbs
- 4 large green bell peppers
- 2 cups tomato sauce

Method:
1. In pan, sauté onion and garlic in oil over medium heat until soft.
2. Add tempeh and sauté until brown.
3. Stir in tomato, thyme, salt and pepper.
4. Remove from heat; stir in parsley, breadcrumbs, and rice.
5. Mix well.
6. Stuff parboiled peppers until almost full.
7. Pour tomato sauce over top.
8. Cover and bake 30-35 minutes at 375F.

Aunt Rita's Casablanca Couscous

Time: 25mins
Quantity: 2-3 servings

Ingredients:

- 1/4 cups vegetable broth
- 1 1/4 cups water
- 2 cups couscous
- 1 pinch salt
- 1 pinch ground black pepper
- 5 tablespoons olive oil, divided
- 1/2 cup pine nuts
- 4 cloves garlic, minced
- 1 shallot, minced
- 1/2 cup sliced black olives
- 1/3 cup sun-dried tomatoes packed in oil, drained and chopped
- 1 cup vegetable broth
- 1/4 cup chopped fresh flat-leaf parsley

Method:

1. Add 1 1/4 cup vegetable broth and water to a saucepan over high heat until they boil.
2. Stir in couscous, and mix in salt and black pepper.
3. Reduce heat to low and simmer until liquid is absorbed, about 8 minutes.
4. Heat 3 tablespoons olive oil in a skillet over medium-high heat.
5. Stir in pine nuts and cook, stirring frequently, until they are toasted and are golden brown.
6. Remove from heat.
7. Heat 2 tablespoons olive oil in a saucepan.
8. Stir in garlic and shallot in until softened.
9. Add black olives and sun-dried tomatoes into garlic mixture.
10. Pour in 1 cup vegetable broth and bring to a boil.
11. Reduce heat to low and simmer until sauce has reduced. Transfer couscous to a large serving bowl, mix with sauce, and serve topped with parsley and pine nuts.

Grandma's Cucumber Salad

Time: 15mins
Quantity: 2-3 servings

Ingredients:
- 2 large cucumbers
- 1 large red onion
- 1/2 cup vinegar
- 1/2 cup water
- 1 teaspoon salt
- 2 tablespoons sugar

Method:
1. Peel cucumbers and cut into thin slices.
2. Slice onion into thin rings.
3. Put the onions in a bowl with the cucumbers.
4. Bring remaining ingredients to a boil.
5. Pour over cucumbers and onions.
6. Refrigerate before serving.

Dad's Garden Grown Acorn Squash

Time: 25mins
Quantity: 2-3 servings

Ingredients:
- 1 acorn squash, cut into eighths
- Several pats of Vegan butter
- 8 tablespoons brown sugar
- A lot of freshly ground black pepper
- 2 tablespoons maple syrup

Method:
1. Place the squash, shell side down, in a baking dish.
2. Add a bit of butter to the top of each.
3. Then, add brown sugar, pepper and a drizzle of maple syrup.
4. Bake at 400* for 30 minutes until the squash is soft.
5. Serve!

Mom's Roasted Garlic Lemon Broccoli

Time: 22mins
Quantity: 2-3 servings

Ingredients:
- 2 heads broccoli, separated into florets
- 2 teaspoons extra virgin olive oil
- 1 teaspoon sea salt
- 1/2 teaspoon ground black pepper
- 1 clove garlic, minced
- 1/2 teaspoon lemon juice

Method:
1. Preheat the oven to 400 degrees F.
2. In a bowl, add broccoli together with the extra virgin olive oil, sea salt, pepper and garlic.
3. Spread the broccoli out in an even layer on a baking sheet.
4. Bake in the preheated oven until broccoli mix is tender enough to pierce the stems with a fork.
5. Remove and transfer to a serving platter.
6. Squeeze lemon juice liberally over the broccoli before serving for a refreshing, tangy finish.

Grandpa Roasted Potatoes

Time: 40mins
Quantity: 6 servings

Ingredients:

- 2 pounds potatoes, peeled
- 1 large yellow onion, very finely chopped
- 2 teaspoons sea salt
- 1/2 teaspoon black pepper
- 4 1/2 tablespoons olive oil
- 3 tablespoons chopped fresh chives
- 2 tablespoons chopped fresh parsley

Method:

1. In a saucepan, bring water to a boil.
2. Add the potatoes. Boil for 4 minutes.
3. Remove the potatoes and place in cold water to cool. When they have cooled off, roughly shred them into a bowl.
4. Add the onion, salt, pepper, 3 tablespoons of the oil, chives, and parsley.
5. Heat the remaining oil in a skillet over a high heat. When skillet is very hot, add the potato mixture, pressing down firmly with the palm of your hand.
6. Reduce the heat slightly, then cook until golden brown.
7. Ease a spatula under the rösti to ease it from the skillet before transferring it to a plate.

Dad's Aubergines

Time: 25mins
Quantity: 2-3 servings

Ingredients:
- 1 teaspoon salt
- 8 baby aubergines/eggplants
- 3 tablespoons chickpea flour
- 2 teaspoons cumin seeds
- 2 teaspoons coriander seeds
- 1 tablespoon finely grated fresh ginger
- 2 cloves of garlic, crushed
- ½ teaspoon cayenne pepper
- 1 teaspoon paprika
- Handful of fresh coriander leaves, chopped
- 3 tablespoons coconut or vegetable oil
- Juice of ½ a lemon
- 3 teaspoons brown sugar

Method:
1. With ½ teaspoon salt, cover the aubergines.
2. Leave them to drain.
3. Put the chickpea flour, cumin seeds and coriander seeds into a heavy frying pan and toast on a medium heat until the seeds pop and the flour becomes darker.
4. Scoop out into a pestle and mortar and roughly crush the seeds. Add the ginger, garlic, cayenne, paprika, fresh coriander, ½ teaspoon salt and bash into a thick, sticky paste.
5. Pat the aubergines dry with kitchen paper, then rub the paste into them.
6. Add the oil in a large frying pan.
7. When it is hot add the aubergines and fry, browning them on all sides for 3 or 4 minutes.
8. Add 3 tablespoons water.
9. Place a lid on the pan and leave to simmer for around 15 minutes.
10. Whisk together the lemon and sugar and drizzle over the aubergines. Continue to cook for a few minutes, turning them once, until there is a thick sauce and the aubergines are almost falling apart. Serve warm, topped with chopped coriander.

Chapter 11: Soups and Stews

The amount of soups and stews a Vegan cook can draw from are endless. Vegetables and soups go together like a hand and a glove. There are many root vegetables that are not utilized except in soups where they neither overwhelm texturally nor with their flavor. This adds a lot of possibility where a lot already exists.

Vegan soups and stews could create a catalogue of cookbooks. Here, we tried to draw from some new inspirational ideas and balance out the act with some traditional recipes to soothe your soul with old fashion comfort. It made sense knowing many of us turn to soup in moments of need, when we are ill or homesick or the weather is dreadfully gloomy.

Mom's Cauliflower Soup

Time: 40mins
Quantity: 3-4 servings

Ingredients:
- 1 medium cauliflower
- 2 teaspoons vegetable bouillon
- 1 oz vegan margarine
- 1 medium onion, chopped
- 7 oz broccoli, roughly chopped
- 1 pint soymilk
- 1 1/2 vegan parmesan substitute

Method:
1. Divide the cauliflower into florets, put into a large pan and pour enough boiling water to cover.
2. Drain, but keep four cups worth of the water and stir in the vegetable bouillon.
3. Heat the margarine in the pan, add the onion and cook over a low heat for 3-4 minutes until softened.
4. Add 3/4 of the cauliflower and the broccoli and the stock.
5. Bring the soup to simmer, cover and cook for 15 minutes. Blend the soup in batches with the milk and parmesan substitute, returning it to the pan. Season if needed and gently reheat.
6. Cut the reserved cauliflower into small florets then add to the soup to reheat.

Hudson Bay Soup

Time: 40mins
Quantity: 4 servings

Ingredients:
- 1 teaspoon olive oil
- 1 large white onion, peeled and finely chopped
- 4 large carrots, scrubbed and finely chopped
- 2 jazz apples, peeled, cored and finely chopped
- 2 tablespoons of fresh ginger, peeled and finely chopped
- 1 tablespoon cider vinegar
- 2 teaspoons ground turmeric
- 750 ml vegetable stock
- Salt and pepper to season
- Large whole kale leaves
- A little extra virgin olive oil

Method:
1. Fry the onions in the olive oil, over a medium heat, for a few minutes until they begin to soften, add the garlic and continue to fry for another 2-3 minutes.
2. Add the carrots, apples and ginger. Mix well.
3. Add the vinegar then the turmeric and mix well.
4. Pour in the stock and cover.
5. Bring to a simmer and continue to cook over a low heat until the carrots are thoroughly cooked.
6. Remove from the heat and blend to a smooth consistency using a hand blender or food processor.
7. Season and gently reheat.
8. Serve immediately with kale crisps on the side or crumbled onto the soup.

Method (Kale crisps):
1. Pre-heat the oven to about 275F.
2. Cut the tough center stalk away from the kale leaving each leaf a 2 slender individual pieces.

3. Place in a baking tray and lightly toss in olive oil. Season fairly generously. It is important to try and keep the leaves separate while they cook so if required split them between 2 trays.
4. Place the trays in the oven for 15 minutes.
5. When this time is up remove and carefully turn the leaves over.
6. Place back into the oven for another 15 minutes.
7. Now turn the oven off leaving the kale to cool as the oven does (this helps them to crisp up properly). Remove and serve as needed.

Grandma's Sweet Potato Soup

Time: 40mins
Quantity: 4 servings

Ingredients:

- 2 teaspoons vegetable oil
- 1 onion, diced
- 1 tablespoon finely chopped fresh ginger
- 1 tablespoon vegan Thai red curry paste
- 1 teaspoon salt
- 1 pound sweet potatoes, diced
- 14 fl oz canned reduced-fat coconut milk
- 1 ¾ pints vegan stock
- Juice of 1 lime
- 1 oz finely chopped fresh coriander, to garnish

Method:

1. In a large, heavy-based saucepan, heat the oil over a medium–high heat.
2. Add the onion and ginger and cook, stirring, for about 5 minutes or until soft.
3. Add the curry paste and salt and cook, stirring, for a further minute or so.
4. Add the sweet potatoes, coconut milk and stock and bring to the boil.
5. Reduce the heat to medium and simmer, uncovered, for about 20 minutes or until the sweet potatoes are soft.
6. Purée the soup, either in batches in a blender or food processor or using a hand-held blender.
7. Return the soup to the heat and bring back up to a simmer. Just before serving, stir in the lime juice.
8. Serve hot, garnished with coriander.

Grandma's Cream Of Tomato Soup

Time: 40mins
Quantity: 4 servings

Ingredients:

- 1 tablespoon vegetable oil
- 3 cloves garlic, crushed
- 2 x 400g tin tomatoes
- 1 pint vegetable stock
- 2 tablespoons balsamic vinegar
- Salt and pepper to taste
- Sugar to taste
- 4 oz ground almonds
- 5-7 oz soya cream

Method:

1. Fry the garlic for a minute or two in the oil.
2. Add the tins of tomatoes, including liquid, and stir.
3. Add the stock or water and bring to the boil, then cook for 10 minutes.
4. Add the balsamic vinegar, salt and pepper and cook for 5 more minutes.
5. Lightly toast the almonds.
6. Blend the soup, return to pan, add the toasted almonds and cream.
7. Stir well, heat through and check seasoning.

Mom's Lazy Lentil Soup

Time: 30mins
Quantity: 4 servings

Ingredients:
- 50g dried red lentils
- 1 small carrot, diced
- 1 small onion, finely chopped
- 280 ml soya milk
- 280 ml vegetable stock
- 1/2 teaspoon mixed herbs
- A little seasoning

Method:
1. Place all ingredients in a pan and simmer for 45 mins.
2. Allow to cool a little.
3. Blend.
4. Serve.

Grandpa's Sweetcorn Chowder

Time: 40mins
Quantity: 4 servings

Ingredients:
- 1 tablespoon vegetable oil
- 2 onions, chopped
- 4 corn cobs, corn trimmed off
- 16 oz vegetable stock
- Seasoning to taste
- 16 oz soymilk
- 2 tablespoons chopped parsley

Method:
1. Fry the onion gently in the vegetable oil until it starts to soften and become transparent.
2. Add the corn and vegetable stock and bring to the boil.
3. Season and reduce the heat, simmering until the corn is cooked.
4. Add the soya milk and blend for a few seconds only, to retain some of the crunch from the sweet corn.
5. Reheat gently.
6. Take off the heat and stir in the parsley.

Grandma's Creamy Pea Soup

Time: 40mins
Quantity: 4 servings

Ingredients:

- 1 onion, finely chopped
- 1 tablespoon vegetable oil
- 1 teaspoon vegan margarine
- 1 heaped tablespoon plain flour
- 1 1/4 parts vegetable stock
- 9 oz water
- 1 teaspoon sugar
- 7oz frozen peas
- 4 oz soymilk
- 1 teaspoon corn flour
- Salt and pepper to taste
- 1 teaspoon fresh herbs, e.g. chives or tarragon

Method:

1. Sauté onion in oil and margarine until softened.
2. Add flour and stir for 2-3 minutes.
3. Take saucepan off heat and add two ladles of vegetable stock. Whisk until completely smooth and then add remaining stock, water and sugar.
4. Return to heat.
5. Stir peas into soup and simmer gently for 5 minutes.
6. Mix soya milk with corn flour, pour slowly into soup and reheat until almost boiling.
7. Liquidize with a blender and season to taste.
8. Ladle into warmed bowls.
9. Serve with herb or garlic bread.

Grandma's Beetroot Soup

Time: 40mins
Quantity: 4 servings

Ingredients:
- 500g raw beetroot
- 2 sticks celery
- 1 large red onion
- 1 clove garlic
- 3 tablespoons olive oil
- 1/2 tsp ground cumin
- A pinch of dried red chili flakes
- Freshly ground black pepper, to taste
- 1 tablespoon red wine vinegar
- 50ml vodka
- 850ml vegan stock
- 400ml coconut milk

Method:
1. Top and tail the beetroot, then peel it under cold running water.
2. Cut each one into eight roughly equal pieces.
3. Chop the celery into thick slices.
4. Peel the onion and cut it into eight pieces.
5. Peel the garlic and chop it roughly.
6. Put all these ingredients into a large saucepan, add the olive oil and stir to coat the vegetables.
7. Cook the vegetables over a medium heat for 10 minutes, stirring occasionally. Add the cumin, chili flakes and a generous twist of black pepper and continue to cook for a further 10 minutes.
8. Pour the vinegar and vodka (optional) into the pan, stir the vegetables well and continue to cook until the moisture in the pan has evaporated away.
9. Add the stock and bring the mixture to the boil. Then lower the heat, put a lid on the pan and simmer for an hour, checking and stirring regularly.
10. Use the point of a sharp knife to check that the beetroot is tender, then take the pan off the heat and allow the soup to cool.
11. Transfer the soup to a blender or food processor and blend until very smooth.
12. Return to heat.
13. Serve.

Mom's Carrot Ginger Soup

Time: 40mins
Quantity: 4 servings

Ingredients:

- 3 tablespoons olive oil
- 1 small yellow onion, sliced
- 1 clove garlic, minced
- 2 tablespoons fresh ginger, peeled and grated
- 1 small apple, peeled and sliced
- 5 cups sliced, peeled carrots
- 2 cups vegetable broth
- 1 can coconut milk
- Pinch of nutmeg
- Salt and pepper, to taste

Method:

1. Heat olive oil in a large pot over medium heat.
2. Add onions and cook until softened and translucent, about 5 minutes.
3. Add ginger and garlic and cook for one minute, until fragrant.
4. Add sliced apples and diced carrots and cook for 3 minutes more.
5. Increase heat to medium-high and add vegetable broth.
6. Bring to a boil.
7. Reduce heat to low and simmer, uncovered, until carrots and apples are softened, about 30 minutes.
8. Remove pan from the heat and let rest for 10 minutes, then stir-in the coconut milk.
9. Pour into blender to fully blend the soup.
10. Once all of the soup is blended, return to the pot.
11. Serve with a drizzle of quality olive oil.

Chapter 12: Main Dishes

These are dishes we want you to get excited by. They are things you are familiar with and love but will experience in a totally new way. Some of them require using ingredients you many or many not be familiar with. In an earlier chapter we discussed what we think of puffy pastries and let's face it, we are too busy devouring to think about them beyond their intoxicating taste. More than one Vegan chef has made the mistake of using the terms *puff pastry* and *phyllo dough* interchangeably, as if they are the same thing.

They're not at all the same thing. It is helpful to know the difference particularly for those who have a propensity for baking! In some of the recipes from this chapter, you will find a few that call for puff pastry. We want you to confidently dive in! Just bear in mind a few fast facts, Phyllo dough is lower in fat than puff pastry. Puff pastry dough is made by placing chilled butter between layers of pastry dough. It is then rolled out and folded, again and again until there are many layers of dough and butter. You can and will do it and you will love it!

Some of these dishes include use of quinoa. This 100% protein grain has been growing in popularity and there is a good reason why. It is light, easy to cook, and mixes well with a variety of foods and flavors because it has not overarching taste of its own. It grows in the high mountain of Peru and in a similar climate in Colorado. Quinoa originates from the Andean region of South America, where people have been farming & eating it 3000 to 4000 years. The Incas saw the crop as sacred and referring to it as "mother of all grains".

Linguini

Time: 30mins
Quantity: 1-2 servings

Ingredients:
- 200g dried linguine
- 500g passata with onion and garlic
- 1 red chili
- 6 slices sun-dried tomato
- 50g pitted black olives
- 1 tablespoon capers
- 1 teaspoon sugar
- 2 tablespoons olive oil
- Fresh basil

Method:
1. In a saucepan in which the linguine will lie flat, cover the linguine with the passata.
2. Re-fill the passata carton or jar half way with water.
3. Add this to the pan. Bring it to the boil and reduce to a simmer.
4. Stir the pasta until soft.
5. Slice the chili, finely chop.
6. Chop the sun-dried tomatoes, add it.
7. Halve the olives and drain the capers, then add all these ingredients to the pan, along with the sugar and olive oil.
8. Stir well, cover with the lid and cook on a medium heat for 10-11 minutes, (stirring regularly), until the pasta is cooked through.
9. Chop the basil.
10. When pasta is cooked, stir in the basil and a grind of black pepper.
11. Voila! Serve.

Dad's Party Pizza

Time: 50mins
Quantity: 4-6 servings

Ingredients:
- Vegan melting mozzarella
- 3-4 mushrooms
- 13 oz ready rolled vegan-puff pastry
- 2 tablespoons tomato puree
- 1 tablespoon tomato salsa
- Freshly ground pepper
- Dairy-free pesto

Method:
1. Preheat oven to 425F.
2. Slice mozzarella and mushrooms thinly.
3. Cut puff pastry sheet into 8-cm squares and place on a baking tray.
4. Mix tomato puree with salsa and 5-6 tablespoons of water to a smooth sauce.
5. Spread each pastry square with a little tomato sauce, leaving a narrow edge all around.
6. Top with a slice of 'cheese' and a slice of mushroom.
7. Season with pepper to taste.
8. Bake in oven for about 20 minutes or until pastry is well risen and golden brown.
9. Remove from oven and top with a little pesto sauce. They are delicious hot or cold.

Method (Pesto):
1. Put basil leaves, 1 teaspoon pine nuts, 1/2 clove of garlic and a pinch of salt in a blender.
2. Add enough olive oil to whisk to a smooth paste.
3. That's it!

Creamy Mushroom Pasta

Time: 40mins
Quantity: 1-2 servings

Ingredients:
- 140g onions, diced
- 140g mushrooms, diced
- 240g tomatoes, diced
- 10 sage leaves, chopped
- 120g soymilk
- Black pepper
- 30g vegan cream
- 200g pasta, uncooked
- Salt

Method (Sauce):
1. Put a pan over medium heat.
2. Add the onions, the mushrooms, the tomatoes, the sage, the milk and the black pepper, stir, and cook.
3. Add the vegan cream, stir it in, and add salt to taste.
4. If you see that the sauce is getting dry, add in some extra milk or water as needed.

Method (Pasta):
1. Cook the pasta as instructed on the packet, and as soon as it is ready, drain it, add it into the pan with the sauce, and stir the ingredients together to obtain the final dish.

Mom's Avocado Pizza

Time: 60mins
Quantity: 6 servings

Ingredients:
- 3 garlic cloves
- 2 large handfuls of fresh basil leaves
- 1/3 cup of pine nut kernels
- 2/3 cup of light olive oil
- 1/3 cup of nutritional yeast
- Pinch of salt and pepper
- 1 Avocado (sliced)
- 1 cup of cherry tomatoes (sliced)
- Pine nuts (optional)
- Rocket leaves
- Basil leaves
- Vegan cheese
- Puff pastry sheet

Method:
2. Place the pine kernels into a large wok/pan and lightly roast until light brown.
3. Put the roasted pine kernels, garlic cloves, basil leaves, oil, yeast and seasoning into food processor/blender and whizz up until smooth.
4. Spread a good amount of pesto onto the puff pastry and top with your favorite toppings.
5. Pop the pizza into the oven and cook for around 2-5 minutes, or until the vegan cheese has melted.
6. Peel and slice the avocado and place on top of the pizza.

Cousin Kevin's Spinach Quiche

Time: 40mins
Quantity: 4 servings

Ingredients:
- 8 oz whole meal flour
- Pinch of salt
- 4 oz cold vegan margarine
- 2 tablespoons water
- 1 lb fresh spinach, washed
- 2 tablespoons vegetable oil
- 1 large onion, chopped
- 4 oz mushrooms, sliced
- 12 oz tofu, pressed to remove excess water
- 1/2 tablespoon dried dill, or to taste
- Fresh parsley
- Seasoning to taste
- 2 tablespoons sunflower seeds

Method:
1. Pre-heat oven to375F.
2. Start with the pastry: sift together flour and salt.
3. Use fingertips to rub in the margarine until the mixture resembles breadcrumbs.
4. Add just enough cold water to bind it to a dough, then wrap in cling film and leave in the fridge for 30 minutes.
5. Meanwhile, cook the spinach gently in a saucepan in a minimum of water, or preferably steam it, until just soft.
6. Heat the oil and fry the onion until it begins to soften, then add the mushrooms and cook for a few minutes more.
7. Either mash the tofu, or blend it to make a thick puree.
8. Add dill, plenty of finely chopped parsley and seasoning. Stir in the mushroom mixture and spinach.
9. On a floured board roll out the pastry, then use it to line a medium-sized flan dish.
10. Pour in the tofu, spinach and mushroom mixture, smooth the top and sprinkle with seeds.
11. Bake for a half an hour, or until the pastry is crisp.

Gnocchi

Time: 40mins
Quantity: 2-4 servings

Ingredients:
- ½ cup red/brown quinoa, rinsed and drained
- 500g gnocchi
- 2 cups green beans, de-stemmed and cut in half
- ⅓ cup green onions, sliced
- ¼ cup fresh dill, finely chopped

Ingredients (Dijon Dressing):
- ⅓ cup extra-virgin olive oil
- 1 tablespoon vegan mayonnaise
- 1 tablespoon Dijon mustard
- 1 garlic clove, minced
- 1 teaspoon maple syrup
- ¼ teaspoon salt

Method:
1. In a large bowl, whisk together the ingredients for the Dijon Dressing – set aside.
2. Add quinoa to a saucepan with 1 cup water, cover and bring to a boil. Reduce heat to simmer, and cook, covered for about 20 minutes.
3. Bring a large pot of water to boil. Drop in the gnocchi and cook until they rise to the surface, about 2-3 minutes. Leaving the water boiling, use a slotted spoon to remove the gnocchi from the surface and into a medium bowl. Drain the gnocchi of any excess water and place them into the bowl with the dressing.
4. Add the green beans to the boiling water and cook until tender but still crisp, about 5 minutes. Drain beans and add them to the gnocchi.
5. Add the quinoa to the gnocchi. Stir in the green onions and dill and serve.

Tomato, Basil and Lemon Zucchini Pasta

Time: 40mins
Quantity: 2-4 servings

Ingredients:
- 2 tablespoons olive oil
- 2 garlic cloves, minced
- 2 teaspoons lemon zest
- ½ teaspoon crushed red chili flakes
- ½ lb cherry tomatoes, halved
- 4-6 small zucchini
- Freshly squeezed juice of ½ lemon
- Fresh basil leaves
- Salt and pepper

Method:
1. Use a julienne peeler or vegetable spiralizer to prepare the zucchini "noodles".
2. Heat olive oil in a frying pan, add garlic, lemon zest, and crushed red chili flakes and cook for one minute.
3. Add cherry tomatoes and zucchini, and cook for one minute.
4. Add lemon juice, fresh basil, salt and pepper and toss to combine.

Aunt Annie's Alfredo Sauce with Zesty Zucchini Noodles

Time: 60mins
Quantity: 3 servings

Ingredients:
- 4 small zucchinis
- 1 cup raw cashews, soaked in water
- ¾ cup water
- 1 tablespoon lemon juice
- ¼ teaspoon nutmeg
- 1 teaspoon thyme
- 2 garlic cloves
- Salt and pepper, to taste
- 1 tablespoon light miso paste
- 2 tablespoons nutritional yeast

Method (Zucchini Noodles):
1. Using a vegetable peeler, remove the skin from the zucchinis and discard. Starting from one end of the zucchini, peel a long ribbon of flesh down to the other end of the zucchini.
2. Turn the zucchini and repeat this step around the entire zucchini, until the core is so small that it is difficult to peel.
3. Repeat this step for the other zucchinis.

Method (Alfredo sauce):
1. Combine the remaining ingredients in a food processor and blend until smooth.
2. Place half of the zucchini noodles in a serving bowl and gently stir half the sauce through it. Repeat for the remaining noodles and sauce. Serve with a sprinkle of fresh basil or parsley.

Grandma's Mac & Cheese

Time: 40mins
Quantity: 3 servings

Ingredients:

- 8 oz macaroni noodles
- ¾ cup raw cashews
- 1 + ¾ cups almond or soymilk
- ¼ cup canola oil
- 1.5 tablespoons cornstarch
- ¼ cup nutritional yeast
- 2 tablespoons miso paste
- 1 tablespoon lemon juice
- 1 teaspoon onion powder
- ½ teaspoon garlic powder
- ½ teaspoon salt
- 1 teaspoon truffle oil
- Pepper, to taste

Method:

1. Put cashews in the food processor and finely grind.
2. Set aside.
3. In a saucepan, combine vegan milk, oil and cornstarch.
4. Bring to a simmer over high heat.
5. Decrease heat to low, cover and simmer, stirring occasionally for 10 minutes, or until cornstarch dissolves.
6. Using a whisk, stir in the ground cashews, nutritional yeast, miso paste, lemon juice, onion powder, garlic powder and salt until well combined.
7. Add the cashew cheese to the macaroni noodles, drizzle with truffle oil.
8. Serve.

Chapter 13: Desserts

Just like breakfasts and dinners, you will find quinoa complements desserts. It is used on only a few of these because of its extraordinary health benefits and because it is an easy ingredient to add to most anything which will make learning to cook Vegan meals go smoothly. As mentioned earlier in the book, quinoa is a 100% protein grain has been growing in popularity and there is a good reason why. It is light, easy to cook, and mixes well with a variety of foods and flavors because it has not overarching taste of its own. It grows in the high mountain of Peru and in a similar climate in Colorado. Quinoa originates from the Andean region of South America, where people have been farming & eating it 3000 to 4000 years. The Incas saw the crop as sacred and referring to it as "mother of all grains".

Vic's Vicious Lemon Sorbet

Time: 45mins
Quantity: 2-3 servings

Ingredients:
- 500 ml of water
- 200 g of cane sugar
- 150 ml champagne
- 100 ml dry white wine
- 3 rosemary stems
- 4 lemons

Method:
1. Wash the lemons in hot water, peel the zest.
2. Squeeze lemons, set juice aside.
3. Boil in a pot the water with the sugar, adding in the zest and the rosemary stems.
4. Let the syrup cool down then, while zest and rosemary may remain there to pull.
5. Once the syrup is cooled, pour through a sieve and stir in the lemon juice and white wine and sparkling wine.
6. Add mix to an ice machine.
7. Stir until froze.
8. Finally serve in a bowl!

No Bake: Black Forest Blackout

Time: 30mins
Quantity: 4-6 servings

Ingredients:
- 80g ground hazelnuts
- 75g dates
- 35 ml of water
- 25g cocoa butter
- 20g cocoa
- 250g berries - fresh or frozen
- 75g cashews
- 60g coconut oil
- 1 teaspoon chia seeds
- 1/2 teaspoon ground vanilla
- 1/5 teaspoon salt

Ingredients (Topping):
- Berries
- Cocoa butter
- Cocoa

Method:
1. Soak dates and cashew nuts.
2. If berries are frozen, let them thaw.
3. Meanwhile, melt the cocoa butter.
4. Add dates to melted cocoa butter in a shredder.
5. Stir in cocoa and ground hazelnuts.
6. Spread the mixture with a spoon evenly over the bottom of the spring form pan.
7. Press it with a spoon a little tight, and then put the spring form pan with the ground in the freezer while you are preparing the next layer.

Method (filling):
1. Warm coconut oil until it is liquid.
2. Place all the ingredients in a blender and mix.
3. Pour the berry mix onto the frozen-pie crust.
4. Refrigerate for two hours.

Method (Topping):

1. Melt cocoa butter.
2. Stir in a teaspoon of baking cocoa.
3. Get the spring form pan from the refrigerator, give a few frozen (not thawed) or fresh berries on the cake.
4. Pour the chocolate into lines on the cake, by the cold of the pie, the chocolate is hardened instantly.
5. Chill overnight.

Grandma's Banana & Date Cookies

Time: 45mins
Quantity: 8-10 cookies

Ingredients:
- 3 ripe bananas
- 2 cups rolled oats
- 1 cup dates, pitted and chopped
- 1/3 cup coconut oil
- 1 teaspoon vanilla extract

Method:
1. Preheat oven to 350 degrees,
2. In a large bowl, mash the bananas.
3. Stir in oats, dates, oil, and vanilla.
4. Mix well, and allow to sit.
5. Drop the mixture by small teaspoonfuls onto an ungreased cookie sheet.
6. Bake for 20 minutes in the preheated oven, or until lightly brown.

Grandma's Carrot Cake

Time: 40mins
Quantity: 6 servings

Ingredients:

- 1 tablespoon vegan margarine
- 3 tablespoons granulated sugar
- ½ cup chopped pecans
- 1+1/4 cups granulated sugar
- ¾ cup vegetable oil
- 1 teaspoon vanilla extract
- 3 vegan egg replacements
- 2 cups all-purpose flour or whole wheat flour
- 1+1/4 teaspoon baking soda
- ¼ teaspoon salt
- ½ teaspoon ground cinnamon
- 1 can crushed pineapple in juice, undrained
- 2 cups shredded carrot
- 1 package cream cheese, softened
- ¼ cup vegan margarine, softened
- ¼ cup brown sugar
- 1 teaspoon vanilla extract
- 3 cups sifted confectioners sugar
- 1 cup chopped pecans
- 1 can pineapple, drained
- Garnish
- Pecan halves

Method :

1. Melt margarine in a pan.
2. Add 3 tablespoons sugar and cook over low heat until mixture comes to a boil.
3. Stir in pecans.
4. Cook until pecans are coated and sugar begins to caramelize.
5. Pour onto a sheet of waxed paper.
6. Break pralines into small chunks.
7. Preheat oven to 350F.

8. In a mixing bowl, beat 1+¼ cups of sugar, oil, and vanilla at medium speed of an electric mixer, 1 minute.
9. Add --vegan-- eggs; beat until blended.
10. Combine flour, baking soda, salt, and cinnamon.
11. Add to oil mixture, beating at low speed until blended.
12. Stir in pineapple, carrot, and praline pieces.
13. **FOR CAKE** Pour mix into 2 greased and floured 9-inch round cake pans. **FOR CUPCAKES** Pour mix into cupcake containers.
14. Bake 30 minutes or until a toothpick inserted in center of cake comes out clean.
15. Cool on wire racks.

Method (Frosting):
1. Beat cream cheese and margarine in a mixing bowl at medium speed until smooth.
2. Gradually add brown sugar and vanilla, beating well.
3. Add confectioners sugar, ½ cup at a time, beating well after each addition.
4. If making a cake, spread frosting between layers and on top and sides of cake.
5. Press chopped pecans into frosting on sides of cake.
6. Press pineapple into frosting around top edge of cake.
7. Garnish with pecan halves.

Aunt Annie's Muffins

Time: 40mins
Quantity: 6-8 muffins

Ingredients:

- 1 ½ cups whole wheat flour
- 1 teaspoon baking powder
- 1 teaspoon baking soda
- ½ teaspoon salt
- 1 teaspoon cinnamon
- 2 vegan eggs
- 1 cup raw sugar
- ⅔ cup vegetable/canola oil
- 1 teaspoon vanilla
- 1 cup crushed pineapple with juice
- 1 cup grated carrots
- ¼ cup lightly packed brown sugar
- ¼ cup chopped walnuts

Method:

1. Combine flour, baking powder, baking soda, salt and cinnamon. Stir well to blend.
2. Beat vegan eggs, sugar, oil and vanilla in mixing bowl. Stir in flour mixture, pineapple and carrots, mixing until all ingredients are moistened.
3. Fill well-greased muffin cups ¾ full.
4. Combine brown sugar and nuts for topping. Sprinkle over tops of muffins.
5. Bake at 350F for 25 minutes.

Raw Vegan Pumpkin Cheesecake

Time: 40mins
Quantity: 6 servings

Ingredients:
- 2 cups almonds
- 1 cup dates
- 2 cups raw cashews
- 2 cups fresh grated pumpkin
- ½ cup coconut oil
- 3 tablespoons lemon juice
- ½ cup raw agave
- 1 teaspoon vanilla
- 4 teaspoons dried cinnamon
- 1 teaspoon dried nutmeg
- 1 tablespoon fresh ginger (or 2 teaspoons dried)

Method:
1. Soak cashews in water for at least 1 hour, then drain.
2. In a food processor, blend the almonds and dates until finely chopped. Add a tablespoon of water if that helps to get things moving. Press the mixture into the bottom of a spring-form pan.
3. Wash-out the food processor and blend all other ingredients until combined and creamy.
4. Pour mixture into spring form pan and smooth out the surface.
5. Cover with aluminum foil, and let it set in the freezer for at least 4 hours. This will harden the coconut oil and set the cheesecake.
6. After this time, transfer the cheesecake in the refrigerator for at least one hour before serving. When opening the spring form pan, gently insert a knife along the edge of the cheesecake, so that it does not stick to the edge of the pan.

Jeremiah Joe's Chocolate Chip Cookies

Time: 40mins
Quantity: 8-10 cookies

Ingredients:
- 1 cup semi-solid coconut oil
- ¾ cup brown sugar
- ¼ cup white sugar
- 1 teaspoon Vanilla
- 1 ½ cups flour
- ½ teaspoon Salt
- 1 teaspoon baking soda
- ⅓ cup boiling water
- 2 cups rolled oats
- ½ cup chopped nuts (we use walnuts)
- ¾ cup vegan chocolate chips

Method:
1. Beat coconut oil until soft.
2. Add sugars and beat until fluffy.
3. Add Vanilla. Add flour and salt and mix well.
4. Dissolve baking soda in boiling water.
5. Blend into mixture.
6. Stir in the rolled oats, nuts and chocolate chips.
7. Roll in balls and flatten with fork dipped in cold water.
8. Bake at 350F for 10 to 12 minutes.

Dad's Almond Chocolate Chip Cookies

Time: 40mins
Quantity: 8-10 cookies

Ingredients:
- 1 cup semi-solid coconut oil
- ¾ cup brown sugar
- ¼ cup white sugar
- 1 teaspoon Vanilla
- 1 ½ cups flour
- ½ teaspoon Salt
- 1 teaspoon baking soda
- ⅓ cup boiling water
- 2 cups rolled oats
- ½ cup chopped almonds
- ¾ cup vegan chocolate chips

Method:
1. Beat coconut oil until soft.
2. Add sugars and beat until fluffy. Add Vanilla.
3. Add flour and salt and mix well.
4. Dissolve baking soda in boiling water.
5. Blend into mixture.
6. Stir in the rolled oats, nuts and chocolate chips.
7. Roll in balls and flatten with fork dipped in cold water.
8. Bake at 350F for 10 to 12 minutes.

Brenda's Fruit Crumble With Ginger Ice Cream

Time: 60mins
Quantity: 5-6 servings

Ingredients:
- 1 pound rhubarb cut into 2 inch pieces
- ¼ cup raw sugar
- ½ teaspoon ground ginger
- ¼ teaspoon cinnamon
- ¼ teaspoon nutmeg
- 1 tablespoon grated orange rind
- 1 tablespoon coconut oil
- ½ cup oats
- ½ cup whole wheat flour
- ½ cup raw sugar
- ½ teaspoon kosher salt
- ¼ cup coconut oil
- Ginger Ice Cream
- 1 pint vegan vanilla ice cream
- 2 tablespoon freshly chopped candied ginger, or to taste

Method:
1. Preheat oven to 375F/190C.
2. Combine rhubarb, sugar, ginger, cinnamon, nutmeg, grated orange rind and coconut oil in a bowl. Spoon mixture into 4 greased 1-cup dishes.
3. Combine oats, flour, sugar and salt in a medium bowl. Cut in coconut oil until mixture resembles coarse breadcrumbs. Sprinkle generously over fruit.
4. Bake for 30 to 40 minutes or until top is golden and juices are bubbling.

Method (Ginger Ice Cream):
1. Ginger Ice Cream Instructions.
2. Soften ice cream. Mix in candied ginger and refreeze until ready to serve.

Vegan Rose Meringues

Time: 30mins
Quantity: 4-6 servings

Ingredients:
- 3/4 cup aquafaba (chickpea water)
- 1 teaspoon rose water
- 1/4 teaspoon lemon juice, or more to taste
- 1/4 teaspoon cream of tartar
- 3/4 cup confectioners' sugar

Method:
1. Preheat oven to 200 degrees F (95 degrees C). Line 2 baking sheets with parchment paper.
2. Combine aquafaba, rose water, lemon juice, and cream of tartar in a large bowl.
3. Beat with an electric mixer until fluffy, 10 to 30 minutes.
4. Increase speed to high and beat, gradually adding confectioners' sugar, until meringue holds stiff peaks, about 10 minutes. Scoop meringue into a piping bag fitted with a round tip.
5. Pipe small mounds of meringue onto prepared baking sheets.
6. Bake in the preheated oven, rotating sheets halfway through, until meringues are dry and firm, 1 1/2 to 2 hours.

Conclusion

It is our hope that with this introduction cookbook to Vegan cooking has astonished and surprised you. We think you will have found out after making a few of these dishes that although eating Vegan is a new idea developed over the past century, the truth is that many foods our parents and grandparents have eaten over the years have had Vegan overtones.

Despite this not being the purpose of Vegan dishes, we hope that you have enjoyed the way our cookbook is composed. We included both new and traditional recipes to stress that anything you love eating now can be turned into a vegan dish. For example: pizza and hamburgers.

We also included Vegan main dishes that are not likely to have been tried before but can be complemented by grandpa's roasted potatoes. The combination is a way of inviting new Vegan foods into your comfort food zone. The purpose of this is that you will be able to make Vegan cooking part of your regular diet.

The blending of both the traditional and the new does not detract from Vegan dishes. It adds to them! It demonstrates to one's mind (and mouth) that Veganism is a natural extension of the human diet. But that does not mean it is not new.

You can eat Vegan once a week or make one Vegan dish a night to add variety to your family dinners. You may be looking for a go-to Vegan cookbook easy to turn to when you have Vegan friends over for dinner. It is not a secret that veganism is becoming altogether more common. A large swath of the younger generations is turning to it and in turn, some of the older ones are, too.

We can see all kinds of signs, from the rise in vegan cafes to menus in traditional restaurants that now offer a limited selection of Vegan options. The same is true of grocery stores. Many of them now have tailored Vegan sections. But eating Vegan food is one thing and cooking it is another.

Cooking Vegan dishes is a bit of a wild ride because it requires unlearning a lot of what you have learned goes on in a kitchen. For those of you who are just getting your feet wet, this book is filled with Vegan recipes that we hope you have found are among the most simple to make. We hope you have found some of the recipes compiled here adventurous and that they will inspire news ways to explore and enjoy your favorite foods.

As always, keep on the lookout for our new cookbooks!

Made in the USA
Middletown, DE
19 February 2018